"Uplifting, inspiring, promising, gratifying, heartening, and encouraging. This book is a tribute to the women who have experienced toxic relationships and overcome adversity thanks to the generosity, emotional and financial support of one woman. I was deeply moved by the inspiring stories of courageous women who have overcome incredible odds to achieve their dreams. Chapters include self-care tips, affirmations, and journaling prompts. These guidelines encouraged me to dream big, practice gratitude and pay it forward. All of us need to dream. Jo's book recognizes and encourages that need and provides tips to fulfill those dreams. It is definitely 'a must read'." —*A Grateful Reader*

"For twelve years Jo Crawford personally helped more than 2,200 survivors of domestic violence achieve personal and financial empowerment. In this book, she combines the fruit of these experiences along with her own journey as a survivor to create a guide for women to thrive in our society. With a heart for the struggles of all women, she has produced a straightforward and easy-to-read blueprint to encourage women to take control of their lives and their futures." —*David Ladd, Founder and Principal, Even Keel Coaching LLC.*

It Takes a Woman to Empower Women

A Survivor's* Guide to Creating the Life of Her Dreams

*We are all survivors!

Jo Crawford

Dedication

It Takes a Woman to Empower Women: A Survivor's Guide to Creating the Life of Her Dreams is dedicated to:

All the survivors, whose bravery and resilience changed my life more profoundly than I could have ever changed theirs.

All the incredibly loyal volunteers, donors, foundations, and corporations whose generosity supported Web of Benefit in improving the lives of thousands of women and children.

Donna and David Ladd, who single-handedly helped Web of Benefit expand our grant-giving to Chicago and twenty-six other states and who became my mentors and dear friends.

Empowered women everywhere who are changing the world in small and large ways every moment of every day.

My family and friends who believed in me before I believed in myself. I could not have done it without you.

It Takes A Woman to Empower Women

Copyright © 2023 Johanna S. Crawford

www.ittakesawoman.net

Disclaimer

In this book you will find many stories of brave survivors who have escaped their abusers. They have gone on to create happy and fulfilling lives. Because of the dangers that these women may still face, it was necessary to change any specific facts that might identify them. This does not make their stories any less true. Every one of these stories, whether told "In Their Own Words" or by me, is an empowering account of how each of these women were able to achieve their dreams and thrive, while breaking the intergenerational cycle of intimate terrorism. I hope that their stories may empower you as well.

Cover Designer: Mariana Coello
Interior Formatting: Mariana Coello
eBook Design: Hugo Herrera

ISBNs:
Paperback: 979-8-218-20968-1
eBook: 979-8-218-20969-8

Synergy Publishing LLC
Brunswick, Maine

"If you can dream it, you can do it."
—Walt Disney

"Well-behaved women seldom make history."
—Laurel Thatcher Ulrich

"You already are a superstar!"
—Jo Crawford

Table of Contents

A Message from Jo

My vision is a world where women can live free of abuse, where they believe they deserve their dreams and can realize those dreams.

I believe we all have similar hopes, fears, and dreams, no matter our race, religion, sexual preference, socioeconomic status, or place of birth. We're all kind and not so kind. We're all fearful and courageous. We're all joyful and sad. We're all caring, and we're all selfish. We're simply trying to discover who we are and be the best versions of ourselves. Many of us have children we would give our lives for.

To be a woman means having to live in a male-dominated society. As children, we accept the image of ourselves as calm, quiet, and well-behaved early on. Gloria Steinem brilliantly said, "It's not only that we live in a patriarchy; it's that patriarchy lives in us." This is so deeply rooted in our culture, like systemic racism, that we don't even recognize its existence.

It is my belief that we have all suffered abuse (in its many forms), sexism, disappointment, abandonment and betrayal in one way or another—some of us more than others. We have been told that we're broken. We have been forced to do more for others and to be less of who we really are to fit who parents, partners, bosses, and friends expect us to be. Author and activist Glennon Doyle says we're "tamed" at an incredibly young age. No more! I hope to walk with you for a moment on your path from devastation and loss to peace, self-love, and fulfillment. Together, let us lift up all women and set them free.

My hope is that you will join me in learning to see a bigger picture; to live fearlessly (but not without some insight into fear); to embrace gratitude; and to find joy in knowing you deserve the best of everything.

In 1640, George Herbert said, "Living well is the best revenge." This is still true today. We all have lessons to learn in our lives: worthiness, patience, boundaries, self-love, courage, gratitude, and, hopefully, joy and fulfillment. Dr. Brian Weiss has said that "earth is the hardest classroom." Don't we know it!

Here are some thoughts I hope you might take with you: Dream big, but focus small. Define your goals simply. Have no fear. Don't let anyone tell you that your emotions and your wonderful thoughts don't matter. They do, and nobody can take them away from you. The only failure is not trying to have the life you want and deserve.

You already are enough. Don't be normal, be unique! Let's make power contagious.

Introduction

This book is not about me. It is about the more than 2,200 women whom I've had the honor to know and walk beside. The book is based on their stories of incredible resilience and bravery, and their dreams of a better life. As such, throughout the book I have provided short summaries of some of their stories for inspiration. These vignettes are my own personal recollections of only a few of the thousands of amazing survivors—not victims!—I had the honor of knowing. Their names and all places have been changed to protect their privacy and safety.

Where you see "In Her Own Words," that brave survivor has generously written her own story so that you can have a first-person account of her journey to create her new life. I am so grateful for their bravery.

Early in the book I will tell you just a bit of my story so that you can understand how and why I came to my personal resolution: that I had to do whatever I could, in whatever way, to empower women to live free of abuse; to thrive and to create the lives of their dreams. I knew that I needed to try to break the toxic, intergenerational cycle of domestic violence.

One of the first steps to doing so is to change the way we talk about domestic violence. To me, the term "domestic violence," has become a cliché. The use of "domestic" degrades the stark truth—there is nothing domestic about it, other than sometimes it happens in the home, where a woman should feel the safest. It also doesn't take into account that this kind of violence, though often hidden from the outside, is the cause of lifelong, emotional distress in those forced to endure it relentlessly over time. It has become a euphemism, minimizing what can be a life-threatening problem.

Instead, I have learned to call this fear instilled by those closest to you "intimate terrorism." It can come from a romantic partner, yes, but also anyone else who is a part of your intimate life.

I will be using this term throughout the book to refer to any kind of abuse in the home. We will also cover the different types of abuse and the lasting, intergenerational effects the cycle of abuse has on survivors, before moving on to how you can take your first steps toward independence and living your own best life free of abuse.

The chapters in this book correspond to the philosophies on which I founded my nonprofit, Web of Benefit, which was dissolved when I retired at age 70. With this book I hope to continue to share those philosophies with you, so that you may benefit from them as so many women like you have done before. Each chapter is dedicated to one of these core beliefs.

My mission is to be with you for a brief time on your journey to reconnect with your innate worthiness and your inherent power—to remind you that despite how things may look and feel in this moment, you are not alone. Together, we will define your dreams and create a unique, step-by-step process for transforming your life. We will dream big, and we will focus small.

Perhaps along the way, we can answer some universal questions together: What is your vision of your best self? What does the best picture of your life look like? What does success mean to you? What is your passion? What is your biggest dream?

To aid you in answering these questions, at the end of each chapter I have added invitations to journal your thoughts and responses to the chapter's topic. Feel free to use this book to get yourself started, or your own personal journal.

Through these exercises, it is my hope that you can come to see your strength for what it really is, and to care for yourself as you would any other person in your life. Thus, each chapter also offers its own opportunity to explore self-care.

How can we get to where we're going without those to guide us? While doing research for the book, I found so many inspiring quotations from powerful men and women—both contemporary and those who have left their wisdom behind for us to contemplate. You'll see I've included some of my favorites throughout the book, with the hopes that you will take what you need and leave the rest. Don't be surprised who you find there!

My final wish is that, when our time together has ended, you will truly believe you deserve the best of everything and know with certainty that you have the power to create it. Enjoy the journey!

Chapter 1

Jo's Story:
Intimate Terrorism

"You must be the change you wish to see in
the world." —Mahatma Gandhi

I don't remember most of my childhood, but the memories I
do have took years of therapy and spiritual work to understand. One
thing I've learned is that although we may be happier, *we usually don't
become wiser and stronger during the good times.* We grow only during
the tough times. I certainly don't have all the answers, but I can say
I've tried to learn from each hardship I've encountered, from each
vulnerability, and from each scary change I've had to make.

Change can be frightening—sometimes it's forced on us, and
sometimes we have to make a hard decision. I know that change, no
matter how it's come at me or how difficult it's been, is also what has
made me who I am today. Knowing that I've gotten through some
rough years has given me the courage to know I can handle almost
anything.

I've never thought of myself as a victim. I've always been too
stubborn. Until I was knee-deep into writing this book, I never
thought of myself as a survivor, either. But I've learned that I am a

survivor. If you're called to my book, you're most likely a survivor, too. Most women are.

I'm hoping you accept *It Takes a Woman to Empower Women* as an invitation to walk together on the same journey and view our survivorship as a story of courage, bravery, persistence, and personal honor. We made it. And every day may be another step on an ever-evolving journey toward safety from intimate terror.

Let me tell you a little about my story.

My first memories are feelings rather than specific situations: constantly feeling unsafe in the place I should feel the safest—my own home—and feeling frustrated, angry, and resentful that nothing ever changed for the better. My parents were emotionally unavailable, for themselves or for me.

I was born and raised in a white, middle-class family in the suburbs of Philadelphia through the 1940s and 1950s. My mother and father were well educated, and we were the picture of what a happy, successful family "should be" at that time. But, like most families, we had our dirty little secrets.

My father was a mean drunk, but oh-so-handsome and charming when sober. I didn't know it then, but I understand now, that he was abused as a child by his father. Up comes that nasty, intergenerational cycle of abuse. My mother also drank, mostly to escape. She had been abused as a child as well, by a domineering mother who ruled her three children until the day she died at age ninety-six.

I Didn't Feel Safe

My house was dark brown with a red door. The black metal letters over the top read "212." The house used to be white with a green door and shutters; I remember liking it better then. Four of us lived in this house: my mother, my father, my brother—who was four years older than I am—and me.

My father wasn't home for dinner very often. He usually came home very late, very drunk, and very angry. At the time, I didn't know why he was drunk or angry, but I did know it was scary. My mother never talked about it, but even then I knew she was scared, too.

Every night, she set the dining room table for four people. She sat by the swinging door into the kitchen, my brother sat to her left, and I was always to her right. The seat across the table by the window was almost always empty.

I have no memories of dinners or breakfasts with my father. We never talked about this. I wondered why my mother kept setting his place, and if other families did the same thing. I didn't know how other families worked, but even though I was little, no more than five years old, it seemed strange to me.

My bedroom was up the stairs and to the left of the big hall, next to the bathroom. I loved my room, except for the paint, which was dark green and shiny: not like our other walls. My father picked the paint, and it's ugly. But the room was large, with three windows and a closet big enough to hide in—which I sometimes did.

I could hear everything in the house. Sometimes it was nice and quiet, but late at night when my father returned home, it would often get loud with the sound of my parents' angry voices. I wondered if my brother heard it, too. He must have, but he stayed to himself, and we didn't talk about it. I would find myself wishing he would come into my room and help me feel safer.

Whenever I woke up to my father's angry voice, I would crawl down to the end of my big bed by the window, suck my thumb, hold my blanket, and listen for my father coming up the stairs. My heart beat so hard as I made myself as little as possible. It felt awful. I would wonder if this was the night he'd come into my room, even though he never did. I didn't dare move.

When I heard him finish in the bathroom, I knew he'd go to bed. I'd crawl back under the covers and wait for my heart to stop beating so hard. I was safe—for now.

One night, the yelling and arguing got so bad that either my mother or my brother called the police. After they arrived, I peeked down the stairs, watching. There were two men in blue uniforms talking to my mother. I didn't see my father, but the policemen said to my mother, "Fix your marriage."

How could they say that when it was my father who was so drunk and angry? It wasn't my mother's fault, but they didn't care. It was that night I realized there was no help for us.

**

As I got older, my father wouldn't live with us for months at a time. My mother had told him to leave, but she was always unhappy, and drank a lot now. Whenever he came back again, I never knew why or for how long. Things would be quiet for a while, but then he'd stay out late again and the whole thing started all over.

I hated this. I never felt safe, and nobody ever told me what was happening. I'd misbehave to get any kind of attention, and my brother and I fought all the time. We couldn't even agree on what to watch on our very first television, so we didn't watch anything. I did get my own radio, though, which helped dull the noise when I tried to fall asleep. I couldn't help but wonder: when would this all end?

During elementary school, I was bussed with my older brother to a school an hour away. Oh, how I hated that bus ride, and my school. It smelled like cooked celery, and the woman who ran it reminded me of the Queen of Hearts from *Alice in Wonderland*; her husband even looked like the White Rabbit.

When I got off the bus one afternoon, I was so excited to be home that I ran to the front door. My brother and I were told by our babysitter, "Be quiet! Your mother is resting." I didn't understand why she wasn't waiting for us to get home like other mothers. Years later, I realized that she drank at lunch and needed to sleep before beginning cocktails and dinner.

By that age, I now understood that when my father didn't come home after work, it was because he'd stopped at the local bar. When he came in for the night, he was belligerent and angry: someone to be avoided at all costs. Often, he'd fall asleep in a chair in the living room.

The tension of walking on eggshells and living in an alcoholic, abusive home, waiting for the next outburst, affected us all daily. Toxic codependency and vicious, predictable cycles of abuse, followed by denial of any existing problem, were part of my daily life. I did not know how to put into words what was happening to us, but I now know it was *intimate terrorism*. We all lived terrified and controlled by the anticipation of what could and would happen next. There was no help for us anywhere.

Attempted Murder

At this point, I was thirteen. My family life still sucked, and only seemed to get worse. I hated school: all the other girls were smarter, richer, and prettier. Worst of all, they had normal families, with fathers who cared about them, came home at night, and went to events at school. Sometimes I'd get invited to other girls' houses, which I loved, but I couldn't invite anyone to my house. What would they think? It left me feeling very lonely, and I couldn't tell anyone.

My father still came and went in his unpredictable way, and we never knew when or if he'd be angry and drunk or sober, apologetic, and charming. The uncertainty was awful, and I still felt unsafe. What would he do next?

He lost his job, and was hoping to get a new one through a friend. But I didn't know if my mother had enough money to take care of us; we never talked about anything. I did know that my father had never even helped my mother buy me a pair of shoes. I was so angry that I even had to worry about this stuff.

My schoolwork was hard, and I spent a lot of time in my shiny, green room, trying to study. I now disliked the color even more. We couldn't change it because, for some reason, it couldn't be painted over. My father had no right to ruin my room. I was a very angry teenage girl, and nobody cared.

All four of us were in survival mode. Three of us were terrorized most of the time, and my father could blow up at the smallest thing.

One night, I had finally finished my homework and was drifting off to sleep. It was very late, and my mother was sleeping in our guest room because she had a very bad back. The doctors hoped that if she slept in traction, it would keep her from needing surgery.

I didn't know how she could sleep like that. She had a wide, black belt that she buckled on her hips, with ropes going over pulleys at the end of the bed. On the end of the ropes were weights that pulled her back and hips down. I guess the purpose was to stretch her back. It looked like torture, and I could tell she was in pain when she was strapped in. Her back pain must have been so bad that she'd try anything. It only added to her drinking and unhappiness.

My brother was in his room across the hall. My father, as usual, wasn't home. I was sure he was at the bar again. I even wondered if he was with another woman.

I was startled fully awake by my dad crashing up the stairs and yelling, bumping into the walls in his drunkenness. He was louder and more brutal-sounding than usual, and I knew he was headed to the guest room where our mother lay so vulnerable in her back traction.

I was out of bed and across the hall to the guest room before I knew it. My brother was already there when I arrived. My father had his hands around my mother's neck, and she was gasping and thrashing her body, but she couldn't really move.

I don't know how, but my brother and I got him off her before he killed her. My heart was racing and I was terrified, but I was also angry. We pushed our father down the stairs and out of the house. We ran back in, locking the door, and raced back up to our mother.

What were we to do now? Our father was a crazy person. We didn't know what to do or say.

My mother slowly unbuckled the belt, like she was in a dream, and walked carefully to her room. My brother and I returned to our own rooms. We didn't talk about that night, and simply pretended it never happened.

However, the next day my uncle flew down from Boston and told my father that if he ever came near us again, he'd be arrested. I'm still not sure who called my uncle that day. Could I breathe again? Could I believe he's gone for good? I felt this had to be the end.

**

After my father was finally exorcised from our home, it took five years for my mother to divorce him. She was still under his control, and was damaged and depressed for the rest of her life. She would live another forty years, and always be fearful of being an enthusiastic, joyful part of the outside world. She became a quiet observer rather than a happy participant.

In later years, she had the options of psychological help and antidepressant medications, but by then she was unable to change. The life she had chosen was less scary than stepping out into the world.

> "Life is either a daring adventure or nothing."
> —Helen Keller

We fall in love with men we think are wonderful, not those we believe are abusers or addicts. My mother was no stronger than the average.

There are plenty of statistics to back this up, unfortunately. For example, it takes an average of seven times for a woman to leave her abuser finally and permanently.[1]

Societal acceptance of abuse certainly didn't help. The final violence happened in 1959, when there was no help for abused women. Even marital rape was legal until 1975. Not only was marital rape not recognized in the courts, but many women were so beaten down emotionally they didn't dare even describe unwanted, and sometimes violent, sexual acts by their husbands as rape. Violence in the home was perceived as normal.

Therapy was not a possibility back then, because going to a psychiatrist would brand one as mentally ill, or worse. My mother, my brother, and I each dealt with our trauma differently. My mother withdrew, my brother took off, and I rebelled, vowing never to be what I considered weak, like my mother.

> "I write for those women who do not speak,
> for those who do not have a voice because they
> were so terrified, because we are taught to respect
> fear more than ourselves. We've been taught that silence
> would save us, but it won't." —Audre Lorde

1. Women Against Abuse, "Why It's So Difficult to Leave," https://www.womenagainstabuse.org/education-resources/learn-about-abuse/why-its-so-difficult-to-leave.

I now know, after many years of therapy and hard work, that my mother did the best she could with the tools that she had. The sadness for me is that she missed most of what could have been a wonderful, exciting life because she was so destroyed by my grandmother and by my father. Her sense of self-worth was ruined by decades of abuse and ridicule. Alcohol became her biggest pleasure.

As I watched my mother live her life, I knew I had to be something different.

The Love of Strong Women Saved Me

The year after our family trauma, when I was fourteen, I entered ninth grade at a school outside of Philadelphia. I was always different: not as smart, not as wealthy, and from a "broken" family. I carried a lot of repressed anger. When I look back on those days, I joke that I was lucky not to have become a felon, but this was probably more of a possibility than I realized. Studies show the connection between future delinquency and criminal behavior and the abuse children experience in the home—whether physical, emotional, or sexual—is overwhelmingly high.[2,3]

"If you can intervene early in the lives of girls here and in other parts of the world, you can begin to change the prospects for the future." —Jane Fonda

Two women saved me: one white and educated, the other black with no education at all. They saved me because their power was love, something an angry teenager from an angry family could not comprehend.

2. Jeffrey Fagan and Sandra Wexler, "Family Origins of Violent Delinquents," Criminology 25, no. 3 (1987): 643–669.

3. As cited by David Hosier, "The Long-Term Effects of Parental Rejection," (2014), http:/ childhoodtraumarecovery.com/2014/01/07/the-long-term-effects-of-parental-rejection/.

Cappy, a nickname for Catherine, lived in a segregated section of Philadelphia. She was divorced with no children and worked for our family almost my entire childhood. She was even there for my small engagement party. She came a couple of days a week to help my mother with cleaning, cooking, laundry, and childcare.

Cappy was wonderful to me, calling me her "Pooh Bear" and letting me crawl into her bed whenever a thunderstorm scared me the nights my parents were away. She knew how awful things were in our home and never said a word: she was just there to help and to love us. I know she's in a better place now—I'll call it Heaven—watching out for and smiling down on me, my daughters, and my grandchildren. I know I'll see her again when I make that trip. I look forward to it.

The other woman I will call Mrs. Warner. She was my advisor and French teacher in ninth grade. I could talk to her about anything, and I did. She was supportive, nonjudgmental, and loving in a way the other teachers at my school were not. It was all about the rules with them, and I didn't play well in the sandbox, even when I was five. Rules to me were often stupid, having no purpose except to keep us "well behaved" and stop us from becoming the strong, independent women we were meant to be. I knew I had to find a way to be who I really was in a time when women were (even) more subservient than we are today.

I look back on those years and love both women totally, even though they have been gone from my life for more than five decades. Therein lies the power of strong, loving women.

Healing Myself – A Letter to My Father

I learned at a very early age that I couldn't depend on any adults to protect or take care of me. My father had terrorized all three of us and physically abused both my mother and brother, and I lived with self-destructive anger for years.

"Life's tragedy is that we get old too soon and wise too late." —Benjamin Franklin

I have spent the past thirty years on my own spiritual journey, which includes thousands of hours of therapy, hypnosis, and counseling so that I could understand and learn from my childhood. I had no words for what happened to me, and it took a very long time to deal with my self-blame, guilt, and anger. I didn't deserve what happened to me. And neither do you.

When I was fifty years old and ending a difficult divorce, I finally decided it was time to write my father a letter: a forgiveness letter. Before that time, I had written an "I hate you" letter that I'd never sent.

To me, forgiveness doesn't mean that I'm telling the other person what they did was okay. What my father did would never be okay. Forgiveness meant I would let go of the anger I had toward him, and no longer let it have an impact on my life. Anger leads to resentment, and resentment, they say, is like drinking poison and waiting for the other person to die. In other words, your anger is poisoning you, and the other guy could care less.

I waited a long time to send the letter to my father, which ended with me saying, "Never contact me." When it was finally in the mail, I felt like a fifty-pound rock had been lifted off my back. I was finally free of my father.

Awakening to My Calling—in My Fifties!

Like so many of the wonderful survivors I've worked with since, no one has, at any time, ever asked me—not that frightened five-year-old, not that angry, rebellious teenager—what my dream was. My life was prescribed by society. Go to college, get married, have children, support whatever your husband does, and maintain a home for everyone. All that seemed enough to me, and at first, I didn't give it any thought. I just checked the boxes. I had a habit of doing things out of order, and I ended up getting married and having two kids before I finished college. But my incredible daughters had dreams, and I was happy for many years helping them achieve their goals.

But eventually, checking the boxes wasn't enough. At a certain age, I can't remember exactly when, I realized I didn't have to do or be what other people or society wanted me to. I didn't need to worry about what others thought about me. The most important truth became what I thought of myself. Was I following my truth and doing what I knew to be right?

> "To think what you want to think is to think TRUTH, regardless of appearances." —Wallace D. Wattles

I was a very slow learner. My big dream didn't reveal itself until I was fifty-seven years old. Better late than never!

By the time I was in my mid-fifties, I had developed a strong calling to do something, even in a small way, about intimate terrorism. I decided to volunteer somewhere I could actually help women. I started looking at crisis shelters in the Boston area and talked with a volunteer director who said they'd be happy to have me come in ... and stuff envelopes. That just didn't work for me, so I called another shelter in Cambridge, and found that they were starting a forty-hour training class for volunteers. The training took several months, and after that, I went to volunteer two days a week at the crisis shelter.

Learning to Pay It Forward

You could say that my desire to help other women who had suffered abuse of any kind led to my dream instead of the other way around. Web of Benefit, Inc. was born one day in 2003 when I helped a survivor who had just arrived with her two young children and two black trash bags full of everything they owned. They had fled on a bus bound for Boston, not knowing a single person, where they would live, or how they would survive. This woman had spent every cent she had on the bus fare to get as far away from her abuser as possible.

That morning, I was in the crisis office of the shelter in Cambridge, where I had now been volunteering for two years. The call came in and, as prescribed, I answered by asking, "Are you safe?" That was always our first concern.

She was safe, at the bus station in Boston. She had been told by the state domestic violence agency that we had a room with beds available for a mother and two young children. She was hoping that she could get in that day. I did an intake interview with her and thought she was a candidate to be accepted, but I couldn't do so myself because I was only a volunteer. I reviewed the woman's application with the house manager on duty, who agreed we would accept the woman and her children.

The policy at most shelters is that no one is told the location of any emergency shelter because abusers, even from out of state, can find almost anyone, especially in today's digital world. I told the woman how to get on the subway to Cambridge and where I would pick her up in my car.

An hour later, I went to the agreed-to spot and found her standing on the corner with her kids and trash bags of belongings. After a very short drive, we arrived at the shelter. I had already cleaned the room she was going to be given, so I helped them unpack, make the beds, and get settled. They, of course, hadn't eaten on the bus and had no food or money, so I showed her where the supplies were for new residents who didn't have their own food. I showed them around the kitchen, the playroom, the bathrooms, and the backyard: everything she needed to know for that moment. I then went back upstairs to the office, as my duty was still to handle the crisis hotline.

An hour later, she came up and asked me if I could help her further. I had no idea what she was going to ask me about, so I said to come on in, shut the door, and sit down. Her kids were in the playroom, getting settled with a volunteer.

She told me just a little bit about her background and the fact that she'd had to flee her abuser in such a rush that she hadn't had time to get their IDs. She had no identification for herself, and she didn't have birth certificates for her children. The reality was that these three people didn't exist legally in the state of Massachusetts—or anywhere, for that matter.

I had absolutely no idea how to take care of this problem, so I asked her if she knew what she needed to do, and she said yes. She needed to request their information from City Hall, and somehow, she knew that it would cost forty dollars. I asked her to let me think about that and see if I could come up with an idea. She couldn't get food stamps, she couldn't get help for her kids, she couldn't get *anything* without proper identification.

Shelter rules are very clear: volunteers or employees are not allowed to give money to residents. And yet usually there is no money allotted for this kind of urgent need, even though the cost is minimal. As you know, I've never been very good with mindlessly following the rules. So, after not too much thought, I decided to take care of this just between the two of us.

I looked in my wallet and saw three twenty-dollar bills. I never have cash in my wallet because whenever I do, it just disappears, and I have no idea where I spent it. But this day, heaven only knows why, I had sixty dollars. It was a sign.

When my shift ended around four o'clock that afternoon, I went downstairs and asked the woman to come to a quiet, dark corner with me. I gave her two twenty-dollar bills and said they were for her paperwork at city hall. I knew she had no envelopes and no stamps, and she would have to buy money orders. I gave her the last twenty-dollar bill to use for these items. "Use the leftover," I told her, "and take your kids for a treat at McDonald's." She burst into tears, she was so grateful. I was in tears myself.

I left and headed home in a nice car to a nice house, feeling incredibly grateful for all that I had. This incident made it crystal clear to me that I needed to do something in a bigger way. I understood that I had changed three people's lives for forty dollars. I had no idea how I was going to do this in a bigger way, but I knew with a capital "K" that I had to do what I could.

Web of Benefit

That day, I saw the huge unmet need to help women financially with their *first steps to self-sufficiency*. I had to do something about this lack in the social services system, but I needed to learn exactly how I could best help survivors with these basic, but inexpensive, needs. Meeting these needs could make the difference between surviving and thriving—or having to return to a horrific, abusive relationship that usually included being held in financial imprisonment.

Because I had volunteered at the crisis shelter for a couple of years, I knew I had to collaborate with advocates at those shelters. On my own, I couldn't find or vet the survivors to know who should receive the grants that I wanted to give. I knew I wanted to help each woman define and fund the first steps in creating better lives for themselves and their children. Crisis shelters don't even have adequate funding for necessities, much less surplus for grants to survivors.

I also had a calling to do everything possible to end the incredibly damaging intergenerational aspect of abuse. I wanted to make my interactions with survivors empowering.

"Empowerment" is an overused word, and not often defined in a way that's meaningful to me. "To give power" is what most dictionaries say, but what does that really mean? I have come to realize that to empower includes not only helping a person realize they have the power to create the life they want, but more importantly, that *they have the power to change the world by helping others*—the mentality of "paying it forward" with compassion. This is the power we all have, and we need to use to create the world of our dreams. Helping others became the second empowering piece of Web of Benefit.

The belief in your own power creates
power." —Mary Pipher

A year later, Web of Benefit, Inc. (WOB) was fully functional and ready to give grants to survivors of intimate terrorism to assist them in creating new lives. For twelve years, I was in the Web of Benefit "dream business," working with more than 2,200 amazing women to help them define their biggest dreams and take the first small steps to make them happen.

WOB was able to give more than $1,200,000 in financial aid during that time. Grants were given for housing, education, laptops, small businesses, green cards, English classes, and even a therapy kitten, each grant individually designed by the survivor.

Ultimately, we decided that a woman had to meet two requirements in order to receive a grant. Each woman had to do the following:

1. Create her own Dream Proposal

2. Agree to pay it forward by helping three other women in need

As you read further, you'll meet some of these incredible women, hear their Dream Proposals, and learn what they did to pay it forward for other women in need.

> "I want to build a community where women of all races can communicate and...continue to support and take care of each other. I want to give women a space to feel their own strength and tell their stories. That is power." —Beyoncé

Working individually with courageous survivors healed me more than I could have imagined. I had no idea that giving forty dollars to help change a life would become my life's calling. How often do the biggest and best things in our lives happen because we followed our woman's instinct to help another woman? I have come to believe that there really are no mistakes. This was the universe creating magic for me. What is magic to me? It's the synchronicities that help create joy in our lives. We just need to be open to life's possibilities and be fearless in our choices.

Invitation to Self-Care and Healing

"Embrace your imperfection."
—Brené Brown

Self-Care: The Neglected Child Within

Lalah Delia, a trauma-informed wellness educator, asserts that "self-care is how you take your power back." Self-care begins with self-forgiveness and self-love, and is accomplished by remembering the neglected, lovable child within us. Self-care is an attitude: a mindset that allows us to put our own health and happiness first.

This doesn't mean you don't care about your kids or your partner; it means *you come first*. Adopting this attitude means that once your needs are met, you can be what you need to be for others—healthy, whole, and ready to happily help those you love.

You may not be used to treating yourself well—let's face it, most women who have been abused haven't learned the art of self-care and don't know where to begin. Start off easily, small if it feels right or large if that's better. Here are some simple self-care activities:

✦ **Prioritize your sleep, making sure you get the amount and quality you need.**

✦ **Watch your nutrition. Learn to eat foods that support your health and energy.**

✦ **Take a walk by yourself. Walking is free and one of the best exercises for mental and physical health.**

✦ **Cook your favorite food. (Not the kids' favorite—yours!) Enjoy it privately.**

✦　　**Paint your nails.**

✦　　**Take a warm bath with bubbles.**

✦　　**Read a book or magazine you love.**

Are you getting the hang of it? These are things that require little or no money and will give you pleasure. I'm sure that you'll think of many more ways to soothe your soul once you get started. **And no feeling guilty!** Treat yourself the way you'd treat your best friend. *Be your own best friend.*

Later, as you learn to heal your wounded child within, you can add, one step at a time, everything else you need to make your life what you deserve it to be.

What have I done to care for the neglected child within myself today?

_____

_____

_____

_____

Affirmations: Positive Reinforcement for Your New Beliefs

Our negative self-talk is constantly swirling around in our heads. It's so easy to believe what we say to ourselves. But you can change that narrative by having some new, very simple ideas to replace the negative thoughts. It starts by being aware of those negative thoughts and saying: "Hey, that's just a thought, and I can think a different one."

This takes practice, but don't give up. It can change the way you think about yourself! Here are some ways to counter negative thoughts:

- ✦ **I forgive myself.**

- ✦ **I love who I am.**

- ✦ **I don't have to be "nice."**

- ✦ **I am just where I need to be right now.**

- ✦ **I can be fearless.**

My Own Positive Reinforcements:

_____

_____

_____

_____

Invitation to Journaling: Writing to Heal Yourself

It's long been noted that journaling—writing your thoughts and feelings—can be healing. I highly recommend you take a few minutes each day, or whenever you can, to sit quietly and get in touch with your life by expressing yourself on paper (or a computer if that's better for you).

Once you get the hang of it, you'll want to do it often. Something magical happens when you write—and we're not talking about "great" or "perfect" writing. Who cares about spelling and punctuation? We're talking about pouring your heart out on paper, saying what you need to say and getting those hidden feelings down so you can release the pent-up energy from your day.

Find a quiet place where you can be uninterrupted for at least fifteen minutes. Grab an inexpensive notebook, a stunning journal, or your favorite digital device and just let the words flow. Start anywhere, and don't worry if your thoughts don't make sense. Just write. You'll surprise yourself!

To get started, here are a couple of prompts for you. Use these to begin, or if they don't work for you right now, just write whatever comes to mind. Keep your writing in a safe place, just for your eyes; or, if you want to share, do so with a safe person (a social worker, a therapist, or a best friend). Please ask yourself:

What really happened to me? Choose one incident and write about that.

_____

_____

_____

_____

What different choices could I make if I were in that same situation now?

_____

_____

_____

_____

What do I need to forgive myself for? One baby step at a time.

_____

_____

_____

_____

How could I be more loving to myself and remind myself that understanding my past experiences is a slow process?

_____

_____

_____

_____

What scares me?

_____

_____

_____

_____

Is my fear based in today's reality or is it left over from my past?

_____

_____

_____

_____

Chapter 2

Living Free from Abuse

"Do the best you can until you know better. Then, when you know better, do better." —Maya Angelou

CORE BELIEF:
Every woman has the right to live free of violence.

One out of every three of your female friends or relatives will suffer some type of abuse during their lifetime. In fact, 43 percent of lesbian women, 61 percent of bisexual women, and 54 percent of transgender women are abused. Also, even more concerning, one out of every three adolescent girls will suffer physical, emotional, or verbal abuse from a dating partner.[4]

More than 10 million Americans are victims of psychological and/or physical violence every year.[5] And that is just what has been reported. More than 50 percent of intimate partner violence goes unreported, which becomes even more disturbing when you realize that 40 percent of all female murder victims are killed by intimate partners.

4. National Coalition Against Domestic Violence Fact Sheet, ncadv.org.
5. Shelter House Domestic Violence & Sexual Violence Center, shelterhouse.org.

All forms of abuse destroy millions of lives daily.[6] It is repeated through intergenerational cycles, as often abusers were abused, and abused women have watched their sisters, mothers, and grandmothers be abused. Neither knows what a healthy, loving relationship looks like.

Abuse can come from family, friends, partners, or bosses: those you most trust. The always-present fear and anticipation that the abuse will happen again is part of why I term this a type of "terrorism." PTSD, depression, suicide, and homicide can be the outcomes.

Victims and survivors alike have suffered the consistent, relentless terror of abuse by intimate partners. Whether the abuse is happening in the moment or whether the ever-present threat of abuse is controlling the relationship, the intimate partner, whom we should trust the most, is the perpetrator.

———————

Choko's Story: From Victim to Survivor

Choko was a doctor in her own country who was brought to Boston by an abusive husband. Because of the extreme physical and psychological abuse she suffered, she fled and went into hiding with her young son. She didn't speak English, and had been so violently beaten around the head that her damaged short-term memory kept her from learning the language.

Her son, meanwhile, hated her for taking him away from his rich father and putting him in public housing thousands of miles from his home and his friends. He didn't care about his mother's struggles, or understand that she lived in fear that

6. National Network to End Domestic Violence Fact Sheet, nnedv.org.

her husband would find them and kill them. He only knew that he was bullied and beaten where they now lived. Both he and his mother were too frightened to go out after dark.

Local free English classes were Choko's only hope of getting a job and moving out of the housing project. However, there was no agency in Boston to help her with the transportation costs to get her to her classes, and she had no one to advocate for her. She was alone with no support, trying to live on $250 a month and raise a teenage son.

One Sunday morning, Choko watched a television show that talked about a different kind of organization that helped women define and reach their goals, even to realize their biggest dreams. She called me and changed her life.

In Her Own Words

September 2006

❝ When my ex-husband realized I was a person of opposite intelligence and style than he expected, he started to abuse me. The abuse lasted over ten years. By the time I left him, the only goal I had was to get my son away from him because I didn't want my son to become like him.

After I left him, my physical abuse stopped, but my heart was crushed by what he had done in the past. With weeping and Bible reading, I fought for survival. Along with difficulty breathing and memory loss, I had to go to ESL class and deal with financial difficulties daily.

Because my teenage son had multiple threats and physical attacks on the school bus and in our neighborhood, it pushed my heart to a limit that I couldn't bear. With a broken heart, weary body, lack of financial support, and anxiety over my son's safety and his distress, the reality was that I was dying. I knew my need for help was critical.

I called after I saw Jo Crawford speaking on TV. We met and made a plan. My urgent request was for help to move out of a dangerous area ASAP. We learned that I had to have an income to make moving possible. So, I temporarily set aside my educational dream and enrolled in a job training program right away. WOB assisted me with subway passes every month, and this released me from a heavy financial burden. WOB fought for me to get my money back from an unfair housing authority decision. I knew this included fighting for my rights, which had such a positive effect on my self-confidence.

The most comfort to my heart was that someone knew I needed help and Jo Crawford, who was my WOB contact, did her best to help me during the time my body clung to the ground in despair. God says, "For He does not willingly bring affliction or grief to the children of men."

From dying to hoping to get a job, I turned over a new leaf within a year of help from WOB. I still need patience to find a job. I still need strength to help my son with his difficulties and academic achievements. We're still seeking a safe living area, but I believe the darkness is passing, and the true light is already shining. I hope that more survivors of domestic violence heal their broken hearts and harvest their dreams. **"**

Choko's Dream

"A year ago, my dream was just to get out of a dangerous area. With the help and support of WOB, my dream now is to be certified in my job and advance in my profession. I also *dream that my son will be more stable in school and that he'll do well. I'm now an example for him. He is the result of my dreams. I still dream about going back to school. My dream never dies. In the future, I want to write and teach. My health is better without medication. My memory is coming back.*

Web of Benefit was a bridge to bring me out of darkness to see the light. What I know now is that WOB gave me a belief in myself and helped me find myself. I don't have much fear anymore. I'm positive and dream of a bright future for my son. My son has new respect for me through the things I have accomplished and the confidence that I regained. My past was very difficult, but I can handle anything now."

Positive Outcome

Five years after I worked with Choko, she was speaking and reading English well enough for her to go back to school to study math. She was living in a new apartment and happily working at a large hospital. Her son was a sophomore at a major university.

Paying It Forward

Choko pays it forward daily with her willingness to work overtime at the hospital and help anyone who needs it, particularly women struggling with intimate terrorism.

Lesson Learned

Choko learned that if she believed in herself and created a dream with small steps, she could escape old patterns and toxic relationships to create a new life, free of abuse.

Jo's Vision

My vision is simple: I wish to create a world where women can live free from the threat of any kind of abuse or violence. A simple theory, perhaps, but one that will need multiple levels of steps and understanding to accomplish.

I believe that we must teach young girls, from a very early age, that they're equal to boys in every way. We can teach them to be who they are naturally, to be curious, to be open to all possibilities, to be fearless, and to be grateful. They will learn that they are enough. And with that, they will internalize the reality that they're perfect just as they are, they deserve the best, and they have the power to create their dreams.

> Women themselves have the right to live in
> dignity, in freedom from want and freedom from fear."
> —Kofi Annan

It angers me that we still need to define and fight for women's rights. Do we ever speak about men's rights? Aren't all human beings innately equal? Human rights are what we need to speak about. It is not logical, or efficient, for half of humanity to have power over the other half. As Ruth Bader Ginsburg said, "Women's rights are an essential part of the overall human rights agenda, trained on the equal dignity and ability to live in freedom all people should enjoy."

What Is Abuse?

For us to live free of abuse, we need to be very clear about what types of abuse we're living with. Too often, we think of abuse as physical violence. This narrows our thinking and excuses our abusers if they don't fit that definition. The more insidious and dangerous types of abuse are the psychological and emotional forms: they're more subtle and nuanced. Abusers are experts at what they do.

The various forms and stages of abuse are often present in subtle ways, even in the beginning stages of a relationship. Please remember abuse is not just about partners. Family members, friends, bosses, coworkers, and even clergy can be just as dangerous. Remember *you are never alone*. There is always help available, including resources that we will cover in Chapter 7 and at the back this book.

We hear a lot about physical and verbal abuse, but there are, unfortunately, many additional types of abuse. Here are some of the main ones:

- Physical abuse

- Sexual violence

- Verbal abuse

- Psychological abuse

- Gaslighting

- Controlling behaviors

- Emotional abuse

- Stalking

- Economic abuse

- Spiritual abuse

- Ageism, sexism, and racism

I'll briefly discuss each of these to give you a better understanding so you can determine whether any or all are happening to you. Most likely, if you think it's happening, it is.

The first thing to remember is that abuse happens to you—you aren't causing it to happen, *no matter what your abuser says*. It's common to feel guilt and/or shame when you're being abused, but try to keep in mind that *this is not your fault*. No matter what you do or how you try to change yourself to be who your abuser wants you to be, *you are being victimized*.

All forms of abuse are about power and control. Toxic people need a sense of control over their victims. We tend to positively reinforce their behavior by becoming more willing to yield to their games and the chaos that they create to stay in the relationship or avoid the abuse. We do more for them and become less of who we are.

"Being a martyr sucks." —Jo

Types of Abuse

The confusing part of abuse is that it does not have to be physical. Emotional and psychological abuse are just as devastating, and leave no physical marks. This devastation becomes even more complete when alienation from loved ones is total.

Physical abuse is when an abuser harms or tries to harm you by hitting, kicking, punching, or using other types of physical force that cause injury, disability, or death. Assault, battery, and sexual assault are the abuser's weapons of this form of intimate terrorism. Physical abuse often occurs with other forms of abuse and will not stop. This is the wake-up call to get out. Physical abuse will only get worse.

Sexual abuse includes rape and forced sex acts or sexual touching. It even includes nonphysical sexual acts such as nonconsensual pornography and sexting. This type of abuse often denies you your reproductive rights, forcing unwanted pregnancies or abortions on you.

Verbal abuse includes yelling, threatening, intimidating, continuous mocking, and diminishing. Abusers may call you worthless or stupid. They will insult you, demean you in public, constantly criticize you, and blame you for everything that goes wrong. This is only the beginning.

Psychological abuse is the use of verbal and nonverbal threats to cause you mental distress by controlling, terrorizing, or denigrating. You will be blamed for everything. Humiliation, isolation, deception, and gaslighting are all possibilities. Unfortunately, the statistics show that 95 percent of men who physically abuse their intimate partners also psychologically abuse them.[7]

Ask yourself these simple questions to understand if you are being psychologically abused: Does your partner threaten you (whether with violence or other distressing actions), isolate you from your friends or family, control your behavior or monitor your movements, tell you that you're crazy, and/or blame you when you're not at fault?

Gaslighting is a very common, specific type of psychological abuse used to make you feel crazy. It's a kind of brainwashing that makes you question your own reality. Gaslighting slowly convinces you that you're the problem, not the abuser. They may set you up by telling others all the "crazy" things you've done. You may even doubt your own sanity. This is done so cleverly that it's often hard to tell the truth from the lies. Abusers love the lies and chaos they create in your head.

Controlling behaviors include alienating friends and family, demanding to know where you are every minute, displaying extreme jealousy, making accusations of affairs, and even limiting access to health care. Any or all of these are red flags for you that things will only get worse.

7. National Coalition Against Domestic Violence, ncadv.org.

Emotional abuse is often very similar to psychological abuse, but psychological abuse messes with your head, while emotional abuse messes with your heart. Emotional abuse forces you to gradually give up pieces of yourself until the abuser has total control. Abusers expect you to be who they want you to be. When you finally know the truth of the situation, it may be difficult to understand how it happened.

Emotional abuse includes harassment, humiliation, isolation, intimidation, possessiveness, and jealousy. It leads to feelings of terror, desperation, and acute loneliness. You start feeling like there's nowhere to turn and no one to help you. Creating feelings of worthlessness are also a cause of emotional distress. This creates a belief that you don't deserve any better, or that you're nobody on your own. You're told you're worthless, and that no one else will ever love you. Broken bones heal, but it's much harder to mend a destroyed sense of worth and self-esteem.

> "Do not ever let anyone make you feel like
> you don't matter." —Michelle Obama

Stalking is a pattern of persistent, unwanted attention that can include calling, texting, reaching out on social media, spying, following, entering a car or house uninvited, and going to your place of work to cause chaos. This causes terror and threatens your safety. Incredible and unfair as it sounds, a woman who is stalked at her workplace or misses work because she's dealing with her stalker often gets fired from her job, making it even easier for her stalker to find her.

Economic abuse forces you to give up financial power and control, leaving you without financial resources. In order to escape the relationship, most of the survivors I've worked with were forced to give up everything. This is the reason most women stay in dangerous marriages with abusers, especially when children are involved. Living in a shelter and starting with nothing are very scary.

Economic abuse can start with preventing you from attending a job and/or harassing you at work. This leads to forcing you to obtain loans and sign financial documents with your abuser. They may also decide when and how you can access and use cash or bank accounts; demand that you give them money; and/or use your checkbook, ATM card, or credit cards.

Statistics show that 94 to 99 percent of intimate terrorism survivors have experienced economic abuse.[8] The abuser separates you from your own resources, rights, and choices, isolating you financially and creating a forced dependency with no way to escape.

Spiritual abuse denies you the support and connection to any higher power in your life and the ability to get counseling from your religious or spiritual mentors. This is another form of isolation in which you are forced to separate from any spiritual or religious belief that sustains you.

Ageism is related to sexism and racism. Statistics tell us that 66 percent of workers ages 45 to 74 have been discriminated against at work. Even workers older than 35 have experienced ageism. While 72 percent of women say they have experienced ageism, only 57 percent of men have.[9]

Scam artists are everywhere trying to take advantage of older people, especially women. I have personally observed that because I am older, I'm often not taken seriously. This is often unintentional or implied, but it still hurts (and angers) just the same. Instead of being treated with respect for our accomplishments, we're seen as weaker members of society.

8. National Coalition Against Domestic Violence, ncadv.org.
9. AARP, "About Ageism," AARP.org/work/about ageism

> "The same way that racism is a white person's problem, violence against women is a men's problem."
> —Gloria Steinem

For more information on all types of abuse and intimate terrorism, go to:

- NCADV.org: National Coalition Against Domestic Violence

- NNEDV.org: National Network to End Domestic Violence

- CDC.gov: Centers for Disease Control and Prevention

Profile of an Abuser

Nobody plans to fall in love with an abuser. We fall in love with a person we believe is wonderful. And yes, they are wonderful: in the initial, most romantic stages of the relationship. They're wonderful because they want you to fall in love with them, and they know how to make that happen. Here are some statistics about abusers and their victims, provided by the National Coalition Against Domestic Violence:[10]

- 92 percent of physical abusers are men.

- 75 percent of stalkers are men.

- 40 percent of female murder victims are killed by intimate partners.

- 76 percent of women killed by intimate partners are stalked prior to the murder.

- One in three women and one in four men are victims of some form of physical violence by an intimate partner during their lifetimes.

10. National Coalition Against Domestic Violence, ncadv.org.

- 76 percent of intimate partner physical violence victims are female. 24 percent are male.

- Intimate terrorism is most common among women aged 18 through 34.

- 26 percent of gay men and 37 percent of bisexual men are abused.

All abuse is simply about power and control. Abusers are bullies, with low or no self-esteem. They get their power by taking away yours. Eckhart Tolle said, "Power over others is weakness disguised as strength."

Abusers can be charming and loving when it benefits them. They're domineering, always feel like they're right, act like victims, and blame everyone else. They're jealous, with quick tempers that turn to rage.

Narcissism often plays a huge role in the personalities of abusers. They're self-absorbed and care nothing about anyone but themselves. Narcissists, sociopaths (those who show antisocial tendencies, have no conscience, and show extreme behavior) and psychopaths (those who are violently antisocial; show no empathy, shame, guilt, or fear, and take no responsibility for their actions) have personality disorders, and sadly never change. They know what they're doing and sadistically enjoy it.[11]

"Women are required to be strong, then we are punished for our strength."—Gloria Steinem

Abusers use shame, embarrassment, and guilt to control us. They make us doubt our own ability to make decisions. They often gaslight us into thinking we're the problem (or that there's no

11. Shannon Thomas, *Healing from Hidden Abuse: A Journey Through the Stages of Recovery from Psychological Abuse.* (Mast Publishing House, 2016). 10. Shannon Thomas, Healing from Hidden Abuse: A 12. Eric Monroe, *Healing from Narcissistic Abuse: A Journey through the 7 Steps of Narcissistic Abuse Recovery.* (2018).

problem at all), and the lies are constant. They work with threats and fear. Abusers are excellent at manipulating us, without caring about our needs.[12]

Most abuse progresses with small changes that are almost unrecognizable. We're manipulated into thinking there is love in our relationship, but abusers are not capable of true connection. When we look back, we again feel shame and guilt for not seeing it. It is very hard to heal from distrust and a lack of worthiness and self-esteem.

In many cases, abusers have been abused as children. They have self-esteem issues because no one ever took the time to help them understand their own emotional and/or physical abuse. I know now that my father was abused by his father, so the intimate terrorism in my family was highly predictable, *but never excusable*—and never my fault, my brother's fault, or our mother's fault. Add alcohol abuse, an unhappy marriage, and job stress, and the formula for my father to attempt to murder my mother was complete.

The Cycle of Abuse

The cycle of abuse is a universal technique, and abusers intuitively know what to do to keep us under control.

The cycle begins with a loving relationship, until the abuser is stressed for any reason, large or small, and becomes impatient and angry. The abuser cannot control their emotions, and blames the victim for all of it. There may be yelling, demeaning, threatening, and/or physical violence.

The first time, it is a shock, and can be both physically and emotionally painful. The abuser is apologetic, says it will never happen again, and begs for another chance. This is the "honeymoon" stage. We believe the abuser because we've fallen in love with someone who seemed wonderful.

But the abuse does happen again, in just the same way, despite promises to change. By then, we're totally invested in the relationship and believe if we can just be better and do more, we can fix it. We give up who we are and become who the abuser wants us to be ... but it's never enough. It will never end well.

Lasting Effects of Abuse

> "Of all the evils for which man has made himself responsible, none is so degrading, so shocking or so brutal as his abuse of the better half of humanity; the female sex." —Mahatma Gandhi

Adults affected by abuse can experience anger, resentment, anxiety disorders, sleep disorders, depression, PTSD, substance abuse disorders, suicidal thoughts, self-esteem and worthiness issues, fear of abandonment, trust issues, and the inability to form intimate relationships or emotional connections.

Children affected by abuse frequently have emotional, behavioral, developmental, and academic problems. They're more likely to be violent, act out, use drugs, commit crimes, and be abused or become abusers. Additionally, children can experience any of the same effects as adults.

How to Safely Leave Your Abuser if You are in Danger: A Detailed Exit Plan

Recovery from abuse is a four-step process:

1. Escape

2. Find a stable living situation

3.   Achieve permanent self-sufficiency

4.   Obtain emotional support

Escape: The first step, escape, is always the hardest. Getting away from your abuser is the most dangerous time for you. It's critically important for you to connect with a domestic violence agency in your immediate area, if possible, before you make any move.

Start with a search for domestic violence agencies near you. Call as many as you need. Their mission is to help you. Their specially-trained advocates know how to get you to safety. If you're in immediate danger, call 911.

Choosing a crisis shelter or other safe place that your abuser doesn't know about is crucial, so try to make it miles away from the abuser and the abuser's family.

For a detailed exit plan, go to the National Domestic Violence Hotline's online *Create a Safety* Plan page (https://www.thehotline. org/plan-for-safety/create-a-safety-plan/#gf_1) to help you decide how and when to escape. A good plan and the help of friends and family are essential. There are domestic violence hotlines across the country to help you as well. Also, please see the resources section at the end of the book.

Find a Stable Living Situation: The second step is to find a level of stability in a transitional living program, a more secure housing situation with family, or an apartment where you will have the peace of mind to figure out what you want to do next. Your advocate should continue working with you as long as you need help. They know about all the other resources in your area as well. They can help with apartments, financial resources, and even free legal aid. They're experts, and they're kind.

Achieve Permanent Self-Sufficiency: The third step on the road to recovery, achieving permanent self-sufficiency, can be difficult. Web of Benefit (WOB) had the mission to help empower women to succeed in this step, and I would like to now help you do the same.

We asked each woman to define her dreams and the steps necessary to make those dreams a reality. In this book I will take you through The Dream Proposal, a fun, easy life plan that will become the road map any survivor needs to start her journey to full recovery.

Emotional Support: The fourth step is ongoing therapeutic support to help you understand and process any mental or emotional issues. This support ensures not only that you can heal personally, but that the intergenerational cycle of intimate terrorism is permanently broken for your children and for generations to come.

Invitation to Self-Care and Healing

"Trust yourself. Create the kind of self that you will be happy to live with all your life." —Golda Meir

Self-Care: One Small Step at a Time

Start with small steps to improve these four important basics:

✦　**Sleep: Go to bed fifteen minutes earlier. Take your phone out of your bedroom.**

✦　**Nutrition: Eat an extra fruit or vegetable.**

✦　**Exercise: Do simple stretches each morning and evening. Walk whenever you can.**

✦　**Emotional Support: Find one person who truly supports you.**

What Small Step Have I Taken to Care for My Basic Needs Today?

_____

_____

_____

_____

Affirmations: Loving Myself

✦　**I will not apologize for who I am.**

✦　**I am enough.**

✦　**My story belongs to me; I will not deny it.**

✦　**I honor my life: past, present, and future.**

✦　**I believe that when someone makes me feel "less than," this is about them, not me.**

Reasons I Love Myself:

_____

_____

_____

_____

Journaling: Imagining a Life Without Abuse

What isn't working well for me?

_____

_____

_____

_____

How can I change this?

_____

_____

_____

_____

What one thing can I do today to feel more positive about my life?

_____

_____

_____

_____

I imagine myself one year from now. What does my life look like?

_____

_____

_____

_____

Jo Crawford

What one word would give my life meaning today? *Gratitude? Forgiveness? Bravery?* Etc.

_____

_____

_____

_____

How can I live fearlessly? Name three first steps that I can take this week.

_____

_____

_____

_____

What am I grateful for today?

_____

_____

_____

_____

Chapter 3

Deserving the Best of Everything

"My idea of feminism is self-determination,
and it's very open-ended: every woman has the right
to become herself and do whatever she needs to do."
—Ani DiFranco

**CORE BELIEF: Worthiness is a key ingredient all
women possess. We deserve the best simply because we
walk on this planet. You don't need to "do" anything
to be worthy.**

For decades, I didn't realize that I blamed myself for my childhood. Young children don't have the capacity to believe their parents are anything less than perfect, so they think everything that is wrong with their lives must be their fault. If they're not loved, this must also be their fault. Blame and shame go hand in hand with that belief into adulthood.

We, as children, wives, or partners, did not cause what happened to us: our abusers did. We need to begin to question our old perceptions—what is the truth, and what are the lies we were told to control us? We never deserved what happened to us! We're not what our abusers have told us we are.

Self-Worth, Self-Esteem, and Empowerment

For many of us, it's easy to dream about the next big vacation, a shiny new car in the driveway, a beautiful new home, or that perfect job. However, when survival is your only priority, you don't have a chance to dream, or even believe that you deserve to dream. For women who are survivors of intimate terrorism, learning to dream and to believe you are worthy of anything is an important step in building the self-sufficiency needed to sustain one's life.

Women often need help to identify and clarify their dreams and understand their self-worth as mothers, women, and functioning members of society, so that they can dream big, focus small, and achieve what at first seems like the impossible.

When I started working with survivors, I thought I would be working with issues of low self-esteem, but the lack of self-worth is even more insidious. We are so often taught that other people are more important than we are, and that it's our job to take care of others first. Women need to be reminded, and little girls need to be taught, that they deserve the very best of everything, and that they have the power to create the lives of their dreams.

I believe this education is the responsibility of all of us, and it needs to start before the age of five. Anything less is not acceptable. If we don't commit to ending intimate terrorism, we're as guilty as the abuser. We need to say, "No more!"

> "Self-esteem isn't everything; it's just that there's nothing without it." —Gloria Steinem

Self-esteem is the value we think we have and the way we perceive ourselves in the world. I soon discovered that these wonderfully brave women not only didn't believe they had any value, they didn't believe they deserved to have a place in the world.

I learned that worthiness—the belief in our own self-worth—is needed in order to define the specific steps and goals to create our personal dreams. It is my core belief that we all deserve the life of our dreams just because we walk on this planet and because we're all given the ability to dream.

So many of the extraordinarily brave women I came to know had suffered years and sometimes decades of intimate terrorism. They had been taught, through gaslighting and degradation, that they deserved to be abused in every conceivable way. I knew I needed to first remind these women that they *deserved* a better life.

Beliefs are incredibly hard to change, especially those beliefs we don't know we have. Glennon Doyle, in her wonderful book *Untamed*, writes that we're "tamed" by society, family, and even friends. Our wildness, who we really are, is gone.

First, we need to recognize this, and then be willing to do the work to change. Those who want us tamed won't be happy: they will push back against any changes. But this is your life, and your choice. And it starts with baby steps—not overwhelming, lengthy plans spread out over years. One step at a time gets you through to the next mile.

Sophie's Story: Stepping into Freedom

Sophie was quiet and very shy. She had been forced to marry a family member at a young age in a country that had radically different customs than ours. She had been controlled and abused by not only her husband, but also her mother-in-

law and sister-in-law. She did not believe that she deserved any better.

Finally, after her sons were grown, she was able to escape her abusive husband. She knew it was a huge and scary step, but also knew she had to do it. She found an advocate who helped with a subway pass and taught her how to navigate the transportation system. Her advocate also got her into an ESL program and a safe place to live.

She came to Web of Benefit to request a grant to pay for her certification to become a licensed daycare provider. She received the grant the same day that I met her.

Sophie's Dream

Sophie dreamed to go to school, to own her own daycare, and to be financially independent.

Positive Outcome

Sophie is now successfully employed as an assistant daycare provider. She speaks beautiful English, and hopes to start her own daycare early next year.

Paying It Forward

Sophie supports other women with young children through her work as a daycare professional, and hopes to support even more as her career progresses.

Lesson Learned

Sophie learned that she could take steps to change her life, even if they were scary. She just had to take them one at a time.

"Step into life." —Pema Chodron

Breaking the Cycle of Negative Self-Talk

It is incredibly difficult to heal from a lack of worthiness, distrust in one's self, and diminished self-esteem. First and foremost, we all must have self-forgiveness and self-compassion.

Along the way, we sometimes take on an unconscious false identity and present ourselves to the world as someone unworthy of love, success, relationships, and a great job or career. We reinforce this false identity with negative thoughts and self-talk.

Think about the thought created by someone telling you you're "not nice." The thought "I'm not nice" is a negative self-judgment. That thought becomes a belief over time, and it sticks. This belief leads you to feel terrible about yourself.

We *all* need to practice being aware of our negative thoughts, beliefs, assumptions, and expectations. Try playing a game with your head. Say to your brain, "I know what you're doing. You're thinking negative thoughts about me. But *a thought is just a thought*." A thought need not have power over you.

It has been estimated that we have up to 60,000 thoughts per day. That is up to 2,500 thoughts per hour. Many we don't even recognize, but for those we're aware of, we can say, "Oh hello, thought; and goodbye, thought." That thought will disappear in a nanosecond.

Your understanding of where your thoughts and beliefs come from will change those negative emotions. Think of where they originated. For example, my mother would say, "Can't you just be nice?" My own misperception that I was "not nice" can be traced back to when I was five years old, hearing this reprimand from my mother. I wasn't "not nice." I was five, but that thought was embedded in my belief system for more than five decades.

We repeat negative self-talk all day long, and this hurts us by making us believe in a distorted self-image. We exaggerate one word, like "loser," until it becomes who we think we are. This is unconscious false identity. Without observation and understanding, we cannot see these beliefs as misperceptions.

Become an observer instead of a critic. Be curious. Question the truth of your belief. Where did it come from? Parents, partners, bosses? Was it used to "tame" and control you? Try to catch yourself engaged in negative self-talk and practice stopping it. Every time you remember, tell yourself one positive thing that you know to be true about yourself to replace the negative self-judgment. It takes practice to stop that negative self-talk, but it will happen. You'll learn you really are perfect, just as you are. You are always enough.

> ## "We're imperfect, but still worthy of love and loving." —Jo

A Belief Buddy

How will you start remembering you have power and are worthy? The power of having just one person believe that you deserve the best is life-changing. Find a "Belief Buddy," a good friend you trust completely. Tell them you believe they're wonderful and deserve the best, and that you'll support their dreams. This empowers you by helping someone else. Make sure they believe the same about you and will support you. Together you are unstoppable.

————

Ji-Hye's Story: A Secondhand Sewing Machine

Ji-Hye was in her late sixties and spoke no English, but she had a very specific dream.

I met with Ji-Hye and her advocate/translator when Ji-Hye was totally alone and had no money after her abusive husband left her. When we sat down to talk by Skype (since she lived in Florida), she was quiet and very shy, not sure of what was happening. She had been beaten and emotionally abused for years. Talking about dreams with the translator was especially difficult. It was obvious that Ji-Hye had never believed she deserved to dream, or even had the power to dream. Her culture also did not support women's equality or advancement.

But Ji-Hye knew what she needed to do to survive—the one thing she could do—was to sew. Her dream started small with just a sewing machine so that she could work from her apartment.

I countered with, "Why not a tailor shop?" I always tried to push survivors to dream bigger, hoping they would come to believe they deserved their biggest, craziest dreams.

Yes, a tailor shop would be best, she said, but how would she do that? I replied, "One baby step at a time."

I knew her advocate would be there to help her with each step. She had already found a sewing machine, plus the other items she would need to buy. The cost was $500. WOB wrote a check that day. Ji-Hye was in shock. Nobody had ever done anything like that for her. For her to know that just one person believed she deserved her dreams was life-changing.

Ji-Hye's Dream

Ji-Hye's dream started out small: a sewing machine and, eventually, her own tailor shop. What she really dreamed of, when allowed to think big, was independence: her own apartment and no more financial worries.

Positive Outcome

Ji-Hye has her beautiful tailor shop and a new apartment. She is happy and thriving.

Paying It Forward

Ji-Hye's commitment to pay it forward started with hiring another non-English speaking woman and helping her to live free from abuse.

Lesson Learned

When Ji-Hye experienced someone—just one person— who believed she deserved her dreams, she was transformed. She understood that she had the power to reach her goals. She also learned that she had the power to help others.

Taking back your power is a lifetime commitment, and the rewards happen every day along the way. By letting go of old misperceptions, we make room for new beliefs. The power of having no expectations, being able to handle anything, and living with uncertainty creates an openness to all the possibilities in our lives. Each time you say "yes" or "no" for yourself first, you're making your outer world fit your inner self. This is empowerment. We learn that we have the power to stand alone and make decisions that serve us.

I will say again and again—the abuse you've endured isn't your fault. You did nothing to deserve it. Your abuser expected you to be what they wanted you to be. You were forced to give up yourself.

No more!

For more on how to change a belief, look to Gary Van Warmerdam's website PathwayToHappiness.com

Invitation to Self-Care and Healing

"I'm tough, I'm ambitious, and I know exactly what I want. If that makes me a bitch, okay." —Madonna

Self-Care: Learning to Say No

Start with small steps to improve these four important basics:

✦ **Decide you need to be number one! Say "no" for you twice this week. Make it three times next week.**

✦ **Put time for yourself in your schedule—at least 10 minutes every day. This is your biggest gift to yourself.**

✦ **Forget the words "supposed to." That's society telling you what to do.**

✦ **Take a walk for your health and personal space. Walk an additional 100 yards more than you were expecting.**

Surround yourself with people who feed your soul.

Who are they?

_____

_____

_____

_____

What Have I Said "No" to Today?

_____

_____

_____

_____

Affirmations: Loving Myself

✦   **I am worthy.**

✦   **I deserve the best.**

✦   **I am loved.**

✦   **I live in the moment, not the past or the future.**

✦   **I'm my own best friend.**

My Best Friend Affirmations:

_____

_____

_____

_____

Journaling: Unconscious False Identity

Describe your unconscious false identity:

What misperceptions of myself do I think I have?

_____

_____

_____

_____

Where did they come from?

_____

_____

_____

_____

One sentence from a parent or a partner could be enough. Our belief should be in our innate goodness, not what others say about us.
Write a love letter to yourself:

Dear Me,

_____

_____

_____

_____

How often do I apologize? Record how many apologies I make over three days:

Day One: _____

Day Two: _____

Day Three: _____

Is this too much?

_____

_____

_____

_____

Chapter 4

The Dream Proposal: Dreaming Big and Out Loud

"We dream to give ourselves hope.
To stop dreaming—well, that's like saying
you can never change your fate." —Amy Tan

CORE BELIEF: We must dream big and focus small.

As a child, as a teenager, as a young adult, I never had anyone ask me what my dreams were. Virtually every survivor I worked with said the same thing. Whether we're young or old, don't our dreams matter?

To me, a dream (noun) is a vision of something you'd like to do, have, or be. A dream is a form of intention: an aim or plan that needs to be acknowledged and honored. Dr. Wayne Dyer, in his well-known book *The Power of Intention*, says that with intention we can create the life that we want.

I believe that to dream (verb) is to have the intention or goal to do, be, or have what you most want—to imagine something wonderful. At Web of Benefit, my mission was to use hopes and dreams as the vehicles to create new lives for survivors. Now, through this book, I want to help you do the same. I created the organization with the total certainty that every woman has the power to change her fate. The dream gives us a road map of how to take each step. It gives us hope for a better life and the knowledge that we alone have the responsibility for our choices. Once we achieve our own dreams, we can then make a difference in other lives.

As I was thinking about my definition of the word "hope," I found, somewhere in the depths of Google, the idea that hope is a feeling of expectation and belief in a positive outcome. Hope is the great motivator.

> "Tolerance for disappointment,
> determination, and a belief in self are the heart
> of hope." —Brené Brown

Many of the incredible women I had the honor of giving grants to had lost any sense of self and worthiness because of abuse. For them to believe they could have a better life, they first needed to believe they could *create* a better life. I knew I had to walk with them through the process of imagining and planning that life.

I also knew that formulating a life plan was very scary to a woman who was terrified that she might not live another hour, another day, another week. Even thinking of a life plan for myself was a very scary thing. I created the WOB Dream Proposal to be a simple, comfortable design that would be a fun and empowering process to do together. It was even more successful than I had hoped—and it was fun!

Wendy's Story: Dreaming After Years of Abuse

Wendy had lived an incredibly difficult life with years of horrific abuse. She could have very easily remained a victim, taking no responsibility for her life. Instead, she chose to be a survivor. When I met Wendy, she had already come so far, and she knew what she needed to do.

Wendy's sexual and verbal abuse started at a very young age, and years later she was raped. She had two sons and two daughters and always dreamed of finishing college, but never had the time or energy for anything more than her family's survival. After she fled her abuser, she knew she had to change her life.

Wendy had no idea how to begin, but she had an advocate who knew how to help. She contacted me, and we met and created Wendy's Dream Proposal. With that in hand, she received a housing grant and a laptop to help with her education. Wendy knew then that she was a survivor, and that she could change her life by telling her story to other women.

Wendy's Dream

Wendy's dream was to find a better home for her children, to finish her education, and to start her own business in order to better support her family.

Positive Outcome

Wendy found a new apartment and finished her education. After, she began writing a book to help other women.

Paying It Forward

Wendy supports other abused women by telling her own story of surviving mental, emotional, and sexual abuse.

Lesson Learned

Wendy learned that she was no longer a victim, reacting to what was done to her: she was a survivor, doing things herself to create her own future.

The Dream Proposal

"The state of the world today demands that women become less modest and dream/plan/act/risk on a larger scale." —Charlotte Bunch

I was in the dream business, helping women define their dreams for twelve years. When I met with survivors and their advocates to determine grant eligibility, they were understandably nervous. Their futures often depended on the resources I had the power to give. They were surprised to learn that the reason I was there was to have some fun and remind them they deserved the best.

The grant itself, to me, was less important than promoting the belief they were worthy of a wonderful life. Each time, I said, "We all deserve the best just because we breathe and walk on the planet." I wanted them to begin to believe they had the power to create the life of their dreams. Our grant would only be for the first baby step; it was just the beginning. They would have to continue to find ways to move forward, but we *could plan those steps together.*

———

Sunita's Story: Dreaming of a Stable Life

Sunita was a hairdresser in her country. She came here not knowing anyone, but loved her new husband and was happy—for a little while. Very quickly, he became demanding and abusive. After having her daughter, she finally fled to a local shelter.

She, like many other immigrant survivors, did not speak fluent English and had trouble finding work. Sunita was lucky to find an advocate who spoke her language and knew about what we did. She came to us for help with learning English and to find a safe place for her and her daughter. We were able to give her a grant for ESL classes and a small deposit on an apartment.

Sunita's Dream

Sunita dreamed of getting a better job and a new apartment. She wanted to create a happy life for her daughter, including college.

Positive Outcome

By sticking to her Dream Proposal, Sunita learned English, found a job, and began looking for an apartment.

Paying It Forward

Sunita hopes to help other survivors look and feel better about themselves by using her hairdressing talents.

Lesson Learned

Sunita learned that with help she could create a better life for herself and her daughter: first by dreaming, then by doing.

How to Start the Dream Proposal

"If what's inside your dreams wasn't already real inside you, you couldn't even dream it." —Gloria Steinem

Let's create a unique Dream Proposal just for you right now. Let's dream with intention together. Imagine—what does success look like? Your Dream Proposal will include your specific goals, actions, and first steps, as well as what you need in order to start. Start thinking: who in your life will support you with your dreams? Who can you support with their dreams? How can you pay it forward?

To start your Dream Proposal, you must be very specific about what you want. The Dream Proposal is going to be the road map to where you want to be in five years; the more specific you are, the more likely you are to get there.

Begin by looking back over the past six months and ask yourself: have you taken some positive steps or made some positive changes in your life during that time? Did you ever congratulate yourself on what you've accomplished? If not, please congratulate yourself right now! We should all stop and give ourselves credit for what we do every day.

Now multiply what you have done in six months by ten—that is how much you'd do in the next five years! You can do anything in that amount of time.

"Why not you?" —Jo

Your dream isn't about tomorrow, or what is "enough for now," or only what you need. It is about defining the best of everything you deserve. Together, we can create a picture of your biggest and best

life. We will dream big and focus small. Walt Disney said, "If you can dream it, you can do it."

There is one big rule. *You may not mention your kids.* Why? Not because they won't be with you on your dream journey—of course they will. But this is your dream. You are dreaming just for yourself. When was the last time you did that? Here we go.

My Dream Proposal

What is My Biggest Dream?

Describe each item fully, in crazy-big ways. You cannot dream too big! Women don't dream big enough, and that has to change with you.

1. Career

If you don't have a specific career, a great job will do. Be specific. This will lead to something even bigger. I gave a laptop to a Spanish-speaking woman who had completed only fifth grade in her country, and she dreamed of becoming a doctor. She got her GED and started community college. Who knows what she's doing now? I believe that she's a doctor.

_____

_____

_____

_____

2. House

This is one of my favorites. Where is it? What style? How many bedrooms? How many bathrooms? Jacuzzi? What does your kitchen look like? What kind of yard do you have? Want a swimming pool? A dog? A picket fence? What else can you add? *Design it!*

_____
_____
_____
_____

3. Car

I have always loved cars. My dream is a Porsche. But how about a Ferrari? A Lamborghini? Maybe a little convertible?

_____
_____
_____
_____

4. Travel

Anywhere and everywhere. Beaches, mountains. Make a list of the first five places you'll go. *The first one is with no kids!*

1) _____
2) _____
3) _____
4) _____
5) _____

5. Self-Care

Nutrition, exercise, sleep, groups, reading, restaurants, music, therapy, time alone, time with friends, spa days...keep going!

_____
_____
_____
_____

What Are the Steps to Reach My Dream?

1. Current Needs

Do you need housing, legal aid, immigration services, or childcare?
Do you need counseling or therapy?
Do you need help improving your credit score?
Etc.

_____

_____

_____

_____

2. Education

Are you interested in obtaining your GED? Attending a community college or university?

Earning a graduate degree or other professional credentials?

_____

_____

_____

_____

Find online classes to meet those education goals. There are so many that you may even be able to find exactly what you need for free. Here are a few places to start:

- www.educationconnection.com

- www.aarp.org

- www.alison.com

- www.edx.org

- www.skillshare.com

- www.coursera.org

What Is My First Baby Step?

1. What will I do tomorrow?

_____

_____

_____

_____

2. How much will it cost?

_____

_____

_____

3. Do I have the money already? If not, where can I get the money?

_____

_____

_____

4. Can I begin saving a little bit today? If not, what agencies can help me?

_____

_____

_____

5. Who else can help me?

_____

_____

_____

Now that you've written your own Dream Proposal:

- Print it out in big red letters (or your favorite color).

- Put it somewhere you can see it every day.

- Create a dream board with pictures of everything that you want and deserve.

- Visualize, in detail, what you want.

- Now believe, no, know, that you deserve it all.

- Think abundantly. This is intention, too.

The last step is to say it all out loud, *very loud*. Tell your friends and family. Don't be shy; you have no idea where support will come from. Synchronicities will begin to happen.

Don't worry about the "how" your dream will happen, just keep taking those baby steps. New steps will present themselves at the right time. Assume your dreams have already happened. Enjoy the surprises—they happen all the time if you are watching!

Examples of Dreaming Big

To encourage your dreaming, I want to share a few actual examples of women who've dared to dream big.

Betsy

Betsy has four children and still dreams of becoming an environmental engineer. She's just beginning a biomedical certification program, and has nine more months before she'll need to leave the transitional living program where she and her children are living. She hopes to get a job in the biomedical field when she finishes school and then continue on to a four-year college degree for engineering.

Rachel

Rachel will soon finish her Bachelor of Science in psychology at a well-known four-year university in Boston. After, she plans to get a master's in social work. Because she was severely and permanently injured by her abuser, she needs a wheelchair and transportation to get to school. Her dream is to live in Miami in a one-floor home and invite her mother to come and stay with her.

> "There's nothing wrong with being ambitious."
> —Angela Merkel

Betsy and Rachel are just two of the more than 2,200 women who've had the courage to open up about their hopes and dreams— out loud! How incredibly brave they were to be that vulnerable.

We used their hopes and dreams as the vehicles for them to define what they wanted in their lives. You can be just as brave. When you truly believe you deserve the best, nobody can take that away from you. You might fail here and there along the way; you might need more help, but you're strong, powerful, and supported. *The only real failure is not trying.* If you dream little, you get little. But if you dream big, you get big. Dream with your imagination, and believe your dream is already real. Your passion is the most important part.

> "You are here to become whatever you want to become."
> —Glennon Doyle

Invitation to Self-Care and Healing

"I'm not going to limit myself just because people
won't accept the fact that I can do something else."
—Dolly Parton

Self-Care: Dare I Dream?

✦   Be still and listen to your soul.

✦   Use your intuition muscle; it will get stronger every day.

✦   Say your dream out loud, very loud! Tell a friend.

✦   Laugh more, at the little things; start with finding one thing
to laugh about today.

✦   Create a dream board with pictures of what you want:
houses, cars, travel, everything!

How Did I Dream Today?

_____

_____

_____

_____

Affirmations: I Can Dream

✦   I deserve my biggest dream.

✦   I can do it.

✦   I just need to take the first step. The rest will happen.

✦   I am brave.

✦   If I fail, I will try again.

My Affirmation to Dream:

_____

_____

_____

_____

Journaling: How Do I Dream?

What am I really excited about?

_____

_____

_____

_____

What gives my life meaning?

_____

_____

_____

_____

What are my top 3 priorities?

1) _____
2) _____
3) _____

Why are they important to me?

1) _____
2) _____
3) _____

What is one thing I can do to make each of them a bigger priority in my day-to-day life?

_____

_____

_____

_____

What does contentment look and feel like to me?

_____

_____

_____

_____

How do I define happiness? How do I define joy?

Happiness: _____

_____

_____

_____

Joy: _____

_____

_____

_____

How are they different?

_____

_____

_____

_____

Chapter 5

Living Your Dreams: Showing Up with Intention

———

"Every great dream begins with a dreamer." —Unknown

CORE BELIEF: Every woman has a right to create her dream and dedicate her time, resources, and energy toward making that dream a reality.

When I first gave money to help a survivor start a new life in 2003, I knew nothing about the power of the dream—the power to dream big and focus small. I had read about intention as being a strong predictor of what might happen in one's future; however, I hadn't understood that our dreams can become our intentions, and thus have a direct impact on our lives.

During the almost twelve months it took to create and initially fund Web of Benefit, my dream was to help one hundred women. I would have been happy to achieve just that. My background was in finance, but I knew nothing about nonprofits. I knew the learning curve would be steep, but not how steep. Failure was not a scary risk for me. Failure would only mean that I didn't help the women I wanted to help. I wouldn't go broke, I wouldn't lose my home, and I wouldn't be hungry.

I had to learn each step of the way—new nonprofit language, new laws, and new ways of raising money. I didn't even know enough to worry about what I didn't know. My big dream was to help survivors, but without creating a Dream Proposal, I didn't know enough to think about specific goals, the necessary steps it would take to offer grants to abused women, or where to get the money. I didn't have the "focusing small" part figured out yet. I was just operating in the only way I knew. I quickly realized I had to dream out loud, because I needed people to help me—lots of people.

I talked to everyone I could. My five-minute elevator speech became very important. Some baby steps took longer than others, and much of my fundraising efforts failed. What I wanted to do had never been done in the same way before. I wasn't a domestic violence agency or a brick-and-mortar establishment, and no one understood exactly what I wanted to do. I was asked repeatedly, "How can $500 change a life?" I knew $40 could, but that was even harder to explain.

From there, the "focus small" idea emerged, and after learning to take one day at a time, including many exhausting, often disappointing ones, my own dream led to twelve years of hard but uplifting work and 2,200 success stories.

Assume Your Dream Will Become Reality

The biggest part of living your dreams is just about showing up with intention. Try being uncomfortable with a little change—change is the only thing we can be sure of. Take a small risk. I've always worked with a "worst-case scenario" philosophy. What's the worst thing that can happen if I fail? If I can live with that worst outcome, I take the chance. Everyone fails sometimes, many times, and usually failure teaches us how to do things differently or better the next time.

Dare to fail. Little successes become big successes over time. Success is empowering.

> "Do not allow yourselves to be disheartened
> by any failure as long as you have done your best."
> —Mother Teresa

I also try not to be overly attached to whatever outcome I'm hoping for, because often the outcomes are even better than I had hoped. Letting go of expectations and assumptions—which is very difficult to do—allows for surprisingly good outcomes. Just try to visualize what you want. Keep showing up and believe it will happen. The "how" is not important.

Remember to dream out loud. It will bring support from unexpected places, and dreaming out loud makes you accountable, which is a huge motivator.

Don't fear being judged by others. You're doing this for yourself because you deserve your dreams. I love the saying "Fake it till you make it." As Maya Angelou said, "Life's a bitch. You've got to go out and kick ass."

Let's look at a few real-life examples of how a dream, an intention, and a small amount of money can turn a woman's life around.

Renata's Story: Paying Tuition

Renata was living in a transitional living program in New York with her two young children. She was going through a very difficult divorce while desperately looking for housing for her family. Her dream was to discover her "calling." Even though she'd found a job, she knew she wanted to go back to school. She applied to WOB for a computer and future rent money.

Over the next two years, Renata spoke with me several times about wanting to go back to school. She had decided that nursing was her calling. She had succeeded in finding an apartment, getting her children into school, and finally obtaining her divorce.

She decided on a school and applied to the nursing program. She received her acceptance letter and was given twenty-one days to send in her tuition deposit. She could get financial aid after that, but she needed to send her own funds for the deposit. But after paying her rent and the bare necessities for her children, she didn't have the extra cash from her salary. Because WOB was able to write the check to the school that same day, Renata began realizing her dream of becoming a nurse that September.

She still had to work and take care of her children, and she found her courses extremely difficult. She called me several times for reassurance that she deserved her dream and had the power to persevere. It took her years to finish, but she took it one day at a time, showing up with intention and focusing small. She's now a registered nurse.

Renata's Dream

Renata's dream started with getting her divorce, then finding her calling and going back to school. She wanted to find an apartment for her family, and ultimately a house of their own.

Positive Outcome

She has accomplished all of the above (waiting for the house!) and has a nursing degree from an elite nursing school. By showing up with intention, she has her dream career.

Paying It Forward

Renata is contributing to the world "in a positive, powerful way" every day as she supports others, including other abused women in her career as a registered nurse.

Lesson Learned

Renata learned to focus small when she felt overwhelmed by the math and science parts of her studies. Once she understood the concept of showing up with intention one day at a time, she let go of her rigid timeline. Little by little, she accomplished the challenging things that led to the dream she knew she deserved.

"There is no limit to what we, as women, can accomplish." —Michelle Obama

Caroline's Story: Finishing College

Caroline was an advocate working with survivors when I met her. She, like many advocates, had suffered intimate terrorism. Also like many advocates, she struggled financially, as salaries are very low due to the financial constraints of almost every nonprofit. Budgets have been cut for many years, and advocates often need to do twice as much with half as much in order to help the increasing number of survivors.

In Her Own Words

❝ In my first meeting with Jo, I can vividly recall her telling me to "dream bigger." This made me realize I had become accustomed to downsizing and minimizing my dreams. As a result of Jo's encouragement, I actually realized several of my dreams and will continue to do so. I wanted to complete my education and vacation in Hawaii. I also wanted a new car and a better apartment. After receiving $750 toward tuition, I worked hard to obtain a Bachelor of Science in human services. Once I was earning my own money, to celebrate, I took that Hawaiian vacation. Another dream was to vacation in some of the places that my mom loved the most and to travel the world. The original dream was to accompany her; however, she passed away before we could make this part of the dream come true. But, in honor of her memory, I've visited several islands in the Caribbean and will continue to realize this dream. **❞**

Caroline's Dream

Caroline's dream was to finish college, vacation in Hawaii, and travel with her mother. She also dreamt of a new car and a better apartment.

Positive Outcome

Caroline now has a college degree, a car, and a new apartment. She travels to honor her mother. She believes in dreaming large but focusing small, taking one step at a time.

Paying It Forward

She continues to help survivors daily, on and off the job, using the Dream Proposal.

Lesson Learned

Caroline is dreaming big and out loud, and she knows she can create her dreams!

> "What the world needs is masses of women who are entirely out of control." —Glennon Doyle

Winnie's Story: Back Rent Needed

Winnie had been in an abusive relationship for many years. I can happily report that she's now totally free from her abuser; however, before her abuser left, he wiped out all her bank accounts, leaving her unable to pay her rent. Her eviction hearing in court was scheduled in Philadelphia two days after I met with her. There was no other agency that could help her quickly enough to keep her from becoming homeless and her children from being put into foster care.

Winnie had found a new job that would allow her to pay her rent going forward, but she needed $500 in partial payment of back rent in order to negotiate a repayment plan with her landlord. With a housing stabilization grant from WOB, Winnie and her advocate were able to go to court assured that she wouldn't be evicted.

Winnie's Dream

Winnie's dream was to be a nurse working with the mentally ill. She is currently researching schools for LPN and RN programs.

Positive Outcome

Winnie kept her family together in a safe apartment.

Paying it Forward

Winnie is helping women find the resources they need.

Lesson Learned

Winnie learned there are resources available if you just look for them. She learned she was not alone.

The Importance of Making Time for You

You've heard a lot about courageous women working hard, one step at a time, to achieve their dreams, but it isn't all hard work and no play—or no personal relaxation. Living your dream life must include time for you—just for you— to do the things you love to do. You deserve joy in your life.

Leisure time is linked to less stress, less anxiety, and less depression, which leads to better moods and positive emotions. Research has shown that time for yourself can help you feel like you have choices and some control over your life. This feeling can expand into other aspects of your life in positive ways.

Realizing you deserve time for yourself can grow into the belief that you deserve the best in your life in other ways and that your choices matter. When you take time for those activities, no matter what they are, you're expressing yourself in unique and wonderful ways, and opening yourself to joy.

Depending on where you are on your path to recovery right now, your choices for downtime will vary greatly, from daring to take five minutes for yourself to spending an entire day at the spa. And who knows—maybe one day, you'll take a real vacation. It doesn't matter what you can do today; it just matters that you start today. Again, as always, focus small, and add just a little more every day.

Invitation to Self-Care and Healing

"Give thanks for a little and you will find a lot."
—Hansa proverb

Self-Care: Building Time for Me

✦ **Put downtime in your schedule. Start with five minutes each day. Then add five minutes more!**

✦ **Have fun. Take a walk, take a bath, light a candle, read a magazine.**

✦ **Floss twice a day.**

✦ **Connect with a friend. How about calling that old friend from high school and reconnecting?**

✦ **Get the catalog from your local community college so you can leaf through it and dream.**

How Did I Build Time for Me Today?

_____

_____

_____

_____

Affirmations: I'm a Superstar!

✦ **I stand tall.**

✦ **I reach for the stars.**

✦ **I love the little child within me.**

✦ **I let my prayer be "thank you."**

✦ **I believe in my abilities.**

Reasons I'm a Superstar:

_____

_____

_____

_____

Journaling: Envisioning Me

What would I love to do? Be specific; visualize the joy.

_____

_____

_____

_____

What is my vision for myself, in one word? Bold, fearless, free, worthy, etc.?

_____

_____

_____

_____

If I could achieve anything, what kind of life would I choose?

_____

_____

_____

_____

What situation felt terrible at the time, but turned out to be a blessing in disguise?

_____

_____

_____

_____

What step can I take this week towards my dream?

_____

_____

_____

_____

Chapter 6

Taking Back Your Innate Power by Learning to Be Vulnerable

"Owning our story and loving ourselves
through that process is the bravest thing we'll ever do."
—Brené Brown

**CORE BELIEF: Women have innate power that needs
to be remembered and accessed.**

When I began writing this chapter, I gave it the title "Remembering Your Feminine Power." I researched "feminine power" and found that it was often defined as calm and caring. That's not the kind of power I'm hoping you'll remember. Why is power, like so many other norms in our society, based on gender? Why should women's power be defined differently from men's? The answer, unfortunately, is easy—systemic sexism and patriarchy. And we accept it without conscious thought. That reality has always been unacceptable to me.

"One of the things about equality is not just that you be treated equally to a man, but that you treat yourself equally to the way you treat a man." —Marlo Thomas

Each one of us has a responsibility to fight for equal power every day for ourselves, our daughters, and our granddaughters. I don't want my two granddaughters to be controlled by a white, male-dominated society.

Anger and Intuition: Your Angels in Disguise

Growing up in the fifties and sixties, I was taught, as you know, to "just be nice." I was never allowed to show anger, even after my father attempted to murder my mother. I never understood how that was even possible. Those huge emotions had to go somewhere.

Many years later, and after thousands of hours of therapy, a spiritual mentor told me that anger is "an angel in disguise," because it forces us to see that something in our lives needs to change. Otherwise, anger becomes resentment, and resentment kills relationships. Our anger needs to be respected and expressed in appropriate ways.

Martin Luther King Jr. said, "Power is the ability to effect change." By remembering your innate power, the power you were born with, you can change your life to be anything you want it to be. With your dreams and your intention, you can take back that power. I believe that to empower women is to remind us of our ability to change—and support us in changing.

To begin to take your power back in baby steps, dare to be just a little vulnerable, opening yourself to what scares you. You are much braver than you think.

Many therapists talk about "rewriting your story." I disagree with that concept. Don't rewrite your story; be proud of your story. It got you where you are today. You always did the best you could under the circumstances. Your story helped you become the superwoman you are. You're a survivor. You can write new, exciting chapters, starting today.

"I'm a woman with thoughts and questions and shit to say. I say if I'm beautiful. I say if I'm strong. You will not determine my story—I will." —Amy Schumer

Surround yourself with people who support and love you. Choose your friends carefully, and set boundaries about how you expect to be treated. Let your integrity and honesty guide you. You will never go wrong.

Your intuition, or your "gut response," is a muscle that needs strengthening. My gut is often much smarter than my brain, which is full of years of misperceptions and fuzzy memories. When I need to make a decision, I let all the choices sit in my tummy, my gut, and see how each feels: comfortable or uncomfortable. You will know what is right. Keep practicing, and trust yourself.

Don't be afraid to make noise and take up space. Spend time figuring out what works best for you. We've been programmed from birth to do more and be less of who we really are in relationships. As women, we tend to minimize our abilities and strengths so that others don't feel inferior. We need to be more, do less, and not care what anyone thinks. The world will not come to an end if we state our needs.

> "If they call you a bitch, say thank you!"
> —Gloria Steinem

Embrace your anger. It will make you strong. We don't have to have all the answers. We do have to have the guts to ask the hard questions. We all deserve the best!

Lucia's Story: I'm Tired of Running

Lucia was attending a local community college in California. Her abuser had been released from jail, and she was tired of running from him. She wanted to become a motivational speaker for young survivors of intimate terrorism. She was looking for a transitional living program and, hopefully, permanent housing.

Lucia's immediate goal was to get more sleep, as she was working and going to school, and had no time for herself. We wrote a check directly to her college to help with summer school, which was not covered by financial aid. Lucia is living fearlessly, even though she's often afraid. This is her superpower.

Lucia's Dream

Lucia dreamed of starting her own motivational speaking business to empower women.

Positive Outcome

Lucia attended summer school, allowing her to take fewer classes in the fall; this gave her some time for herself throughout the year.

Paying It Forward

Lucia spoke publicly about her story whenever she could to help survivors.

Lesson Learned

Lucia learned that she did not need to be afraid.

Taking back your power is a lifetime commitment, and the rewards of your work empower you every day. Trust your inner awareness and strength. Every time you say "yes" or "no," you're making your outer world match your inner dreams. When you step into your true inner power, knowing that you're enough, you will not be thrown off course when circumstances go against you. This is authentic power. No one can take this away from you. Be proud of your unique self and celebrate your new life.

Fear of Being Abused (Again)

I believe you already have all the power you'll ever need. Saying "yes" to changes in your life allows you to dream and allows those dreams to manifest.

It's very, very scary to be open to choices, changes, and risks, but that's where your power lies: knowing that you truly deserve whatever brings you joy. You must look for your passion because passion makes us fearless.

Fear comes in many different forms. Fear of failure is often damaging for survivors of spousal abuse, as they feel they have failed at their most important relationship, a relationship they believed they could depend on. Fear of being abused again keeps them from feeling safe in the world and from trusting others to treat them fairly.

My fear of writing this book has led me to look for any distraction possible to avoid doing it. Who am I to write a book? I would rather wash the floor, clean the house, mow the lawn, or do practically anything instead of putting myself out there and pretending that I should, or even could, write a book.

Our sense of worthiness can make the difference. It allows us to embrace all the possibilities in our life knowing that we, too, deserve the best. We need not be limited in our dreams or in our reality. We just need to ask our future selves what we want.

> "Always remember, you have within you the strength, the patience, and the passion to reach for the stars, to change the world." —Harriet Tubman

To remember our power, we must be willing to love ourselves with no shame, blame, or guilt. This would be a big, beautiful change for all of us. Let's take a look at authentic examples of women who have found their inner power source and are practicing being vulnerable enough to take small steps to confront their fear and embrace their power.

Henrietta's Story: Becoming a Doctor

Henrietta had been in a shelter in Arizona for more than six months with her young son. She had trained and worked as a nurse in Ghana. Fleeing an abusive marriage, she sought safety in the US and had come here from Africa with nothing.

She wanted to become a nurse's aide, but like many women from foreign countries, she did not have her necessary educational credentials. She applied to WOB and received a laptop. With it, she was able to contact family and friends and get her records from Ghana. She began researching her options to pursue her nursing license here.

Henrietta is an exceptional example of what believing in a dream and support from just one person can do to help her succeed in her goals. She can now stay in touch with her family and research job and educational opportunities.

Henrietta's Dream

Henrietta's dream was to get her own apartment and become a doctor.

Positive Outcome

By reaching out for help, Henrietta received the documents she needed from Ghana to start a life in the United States. This first step enabled her to move forward and become a nurse.

Paying It Forward

Because Henrietta received a laptop, she was able to help other women at the shelter find housing and jobs.

Lesson Learned

After she opened up to us, Henrietta was shocked to learn that her advocate and I believed she could accomplish whatever she wanted. She began believing it herself.

"What am I grateful for today?" —Jo

Alejandra's Story: A Harrowing Escape

Alejandra is the one and only woman I ever helped leave her abuser. I had no choice, as I knew she would be killed if she didn't flee. I was just as scared as she was. I remember how sad I was that she had to leave her beautiful dog. Her story is the same for millions of women who fall in love with men they think are wonderful. Abusers are terrific actors, often crying, apologizing, and promising to change.

I've known Alejandra for fourteen years now. She owns her own home, loves her job, and her small daughter is now a sophomore in college. I count her among my good friends.

In Her Own Words

My grant was given in late 2008.

❝ It's hard to accept even now that I'm a domestic violence survivor. I guess I always saw myself as a strong and independent woman. I had an education, a career, and a wonderful network of family and friends back in my home country. I was a proud single parent carrying on with life successfully. It all changed in 2006 when I met a man at the beach I thought was wonderful. He was visiting, and oh, he was charming! All smiles and fun. We had a great weekend together that ended with promises of staying in touch. I honestly didn't think it would come this far, but that's probably because I was in my early twenties. He had eight years on me and a whole master plan.

We dated long-distance for about a year until we finally made the difficult decision for me to move to the US so we could be together. I say difficult because I had to leave my daughter behind with her grandparents, at least for the try-out period, and while her immigration paperwork was processed. We were married by 2007. A few months in—I guess you could call that a very short honeymoon period— things began to change. This very charming, protective, and sweet guy quickly transformed into someone controlling, aggressive, and moody.

Once I was under his "care" in a foreign country, he didn't have to pretend to be nice anymore. I endured so much, but because he never actually hit me, I never believed it was abuse. I was controlled in every aspect of my life: driven to and picked up from work, and sex on demand. He controlled my weight and eating portions, all bills and expenses, and when I was allowed to fly back home. Although I was working, I had no autonomy or financial say in our matters. I tried to fight back by arguing and standing up for myself, but he usually threatened me with immigration warnings. He would say, "If you don't listen to me or do as I ask, I'll stop your immigration process and your daughter's." He certainly made sure to strongly state who was in charge of our future. I felt like a house pet, like a piece of furniture to decorate the house. I was losing all sense of self, and I didn't have anyone to talk to.

As often predicted, his behavior escalated to the point of pushing me around, throwing things at me, and calling me names nonstop. He would then cry, apologize, and admit he had a problem, but he'd never do anything to change. He always made sure to say he acted irrationally because of love. I lived trapped in this cycle for a little over a year. I was so depressed, but I knew I had to do something to get out.

With my daughter in mind, I set a goal to hide money from him as part of an escape plan. I was determined to stay in the country and bring my daughter in, but I couldn't do it while I was still with him. I refused to bring her into this mess.

My dream was to be free, to begin again with my daughter by my side.

The last fight we had is the one that actually saved me. He lost control again over some insignificant reason. It was one of those horrible fights that lasted all afternoon and into the night. He would follow me around the house, yell at me, and repeat himself over and over. I was not allowed to eat that night or use electricity. I complied and cried myself to sleep. The next day, he drove me to work as was our normal routine. He apologized plenty of times in the car, of course, but I was done listening. When I arrived at my office, I think my boss was suspicious that something was going on in my life, as I often arrived tired and teary-eyed. Thank God he had the nerve to ask me if everything was all right that day. Like a bubble ready to burst, I just began crying in his office and explained everything I had endured the last year. His kind soul was horrified. He immediately began making calls to make sure I received support.

Jo came to our office within a couple of hours. She was kind, fierce, and ready to take action. After some information exchange, she realized I had already begun the process of "leaving," as I had been saving and had made contact with some friends in another city for potential housing. She then asked me what I needed to make a move. To my surprise, all I said was, "Um, I don't have suitcases, and I need a one-way plane ticket." Jo smiled and told me to consider it done. I also began making calls to secure a place to stay in my new city.

We had only a couple of hours to get to my husband's apartment before the workday ended. Jo drove me there, and like a bodyguard, stood by the door waiting for me to gather my things. I was frantic, somewhere between terrified and relieved. Jo then made sure I was in a safe place that night and sent me off to my new life the next morning. New suitcases and all.

I still can't believe this happened ten years ago. My life changed that afternoon when my boss and Jo intervened. I'm still unsure to this day if I ever would have gathered the strength to leave without them. That conversation and grant changed my life. I needed that push. I needed someone to tell me "It will be ok—you will make it. We got you."

My daughter moved to the US in 2009. I finalized my divorce a few months later. And as part of my promise to help other women, I worked in nonprofits related to domestic violence and volunteered for WOB in my new city. Consequently, I completed a master's degree in counseling. I'm now a licensed mental health therapist and a high school counselor helping and empowering women and teens. I'm still a single parent. I'm still a strong, independent, and courageous woman. I'm raising my daughter, now a teen, to believe in herself. I have taught her that female empowerment is not about fitting in the glass slipper but breaking glass ceilings. I'm forever grateful to WOB and my network of family and friends for reminding me back then that I deserved happiness. 🟊🟊

Alejandra's Dream

Alejandra dreamed to begin again, free with her daughter by her side.

Positive Outcome

Alejandra recognized and acknowledged that she's a strong, independent, and courageous woman no matter what kind of abusive history she's lived through.

Paying It Forward

As part of her promise to help other women, Alejandra worked in nonprofits related to domestic violence. She has made a commitment to always pay it forward whenever the opportunity to help another abused woman arises.

Lessons Learned

Life is amazing, and people will surprise you—help can come from any corner if you open yourself up to it!

More Thoughts about Power

When you're remembering your power, try not to think or say "I should," "I can't," "I never," or "I always." Our constant negative self-talk is a damaging perspective that holds us back. Start to believe in abundance: it's much more fun than fearing lack.

Power takes many different forms. Bullies, abusers, narcissists, sociopaths, and psychopaths all instinctively know how to use power to harm others. They create chaos and doubt. They control through implicit and explicit threats using coercive power, and they reward your obedience by giving you small moments of happiness and love. This isn't love; it's manipulation, power, and control.

I believe that real power is born from respect and empathy, from compassionate communication and love. People with real power empower others. That was the core mission of Web of Benefit, and it's the core mission of this book.

You have already done the hardest part and started on your path to recovery. Be patient with yourself. Be open to everything. Give yourself credit for what you've accomplished. You already have all the power you'll ever need. Congratulations!

Invitation to Self-Care and Healing

"Control stops the magic."
—Belinda Womack

Self-Care: Practice Being Vulnerable

✦   **Tell someone what you need.**

✦   **Take up more space.**

✦   **Do one thing that's a little scary for you today.**

✦   **Do one thing today to put yourself first.**

✦   **Share your story. You are important.**

What Have I Done That Made Me Vulnerable Today?

_____

_____

_____

_____

Affirmations: Practice Being Fearless

✦   **I practice self-acceptance and self-love.**

✦   **I trust my intuition.**

✦   **I'm willing to take risks, even little ones.**

✦   **I'm becoming the person I want and deserve to be.**

✦   **I'm on my own unique journey.**

Ways I am Fearless:

Journaling: Answering the Great Healing Questions to Regain Your Power

What is one thing I do well?

_____
_____
_____
_____

What is one thing I do that takes courage?

_____
_____
_____
_____

What is one more thing I can start doing courageously?

_____
_____
_____
_____

What am I grateful for today?

_____
_____
_____
_____

What is one thing I do that is authentically me?

_____

_____

_____

_____

What is one more thing I can start doing authentically?

_____

_____

_____

_____

What fears are stopping me?

_____

_____

_____

_____

Are they real or are they a misperception?

_____

_____

_____

_____

Chapter 7

Reclaiming Your Economic Independence and Breaking the Cycle of Domestic Violence

"Wholehearted living is about engaging in our lives from a place of worthiness." —Brené Brown

CORE BELIEF: Women need both emotional and financial support to reclaim their power, become economically independent, and break the intergenerational cycle of domestic violence.

No matter where you are on your path to recovery and empowerment, real independence includes some level of financial security. *Fear of financial insecurity is the main reason women stay in abusive relationships.* This is a real fear, and it takes a huge amount of courage to run, with or without children, not knowing how you'll survive. According to CNBC, a minimally-comfortable life for a mother and two children costs an average of more than $56,000 per year in Oklahoma, and more than $74,000 in California. How does a survivor begin to earn that amount of money? How does she begin to believe she *deserves* to earn that amount of money?

Again, this is where worthiness comes in. Believing you deserve to earn the money and live that kind of life is the first step. The second step, of course, is creating the dream, which really is your intention of how you will succeed in creating the life that you want along with your financial independence.

Remember, although it sounds contradictory, the first steps towards independence don't cost huge amounts of money. Often, the first step leads to the next one.

––––––––––

Marie's Story: Freedom from Substance Abuse

I met Marie at a coffee shop in the town where she grew up. She was young, well-educated, and just beginning to believe she deserved something more in her life. She was still recovering slowly from abuse and addiction, but was positive she could change her life for the better. She was one of the lucky ones who already had an education and a support system in place. She had already done a huge amount of inner work to remain sober, and was ready to be on her own.

Marie admitted that she had spent so many years "just surviving" that she never thought to dream. She needed help to pay for her certificate in substance-abuse counseling, which we gave to her. She was able to begin saving money again and to look for a small apartment of her own.

Marie's Dream

Marie's dream was to obtain her substance-abuse counseling certificate and to live in her own apartment. She wanted independence.

Positive Outcome

Marie has her freedom: from addiction, from abuse, and from dependency. She now has her counseling certificate and a life plan.

Paying It Forward

Marie uses her degree and substance-abuse counseling certificate to support other abused and addicted women. She helps them find the same independence she has gained.

Lesson Learned

Marie learned that she deserved more in her life, and that she had the tools she needed to take those first steps towards her own independence.

Gaining a Financial Start to Independence

Finding advocates, agencies, and mentors to help you is just as important as the money. They are there to help you in every state. Domestic violence agencies will help you if you're just beginning on your path to independence and empowerment. Even if you don't live in their shelters, they have advocates who work in the community and have extensive knowledge of and access to local and federal resources.

There is information about financial aid programs at these key organizations:

- Growing Family Benefits: www.growingfamilybenefits.com.

- Single Mothers Grants: www.singlemothersgrants.org.

- One Parent: www.oneparent.org.

There are all sorts of job-training programs that you can find on the Department of Labor website (www.dol.gov). All you need to do is Google "free education." Most cities have a Department of Women's Affairs or something comparable. You can certainly start there.

Rather than finding work elsewhere, many of our grantees started their own small businesses: catering, food carts, restaurants, hair salons, public speaking, daycares, tailoring, and so forth. If you're creative, you can start a free (or relatively inexpensive) account on Etsy (www.etsy.com).

"Women belong in all places where decisions are being made. It shouldn't be that women are the exception."
—Ruth Bader Ginsberg

The unfortunate truth is that, on average, women earn only 82 percent of men's salaries. As stated at www.census.gov, for female lawyers, it's only 78 percent. Are male lawyers 22 percent better than female lawyers? No, of course not, but female lawyers with children often find it difficult to work sixty hours a week if their partners are not doing 50 percent of the childcare and housework. Women are often expected to do it all!

Some of this pay inequality is finally beginning to change. Recently, the National Women's Soccer League won a $24 million settlement for back pay, and was promised equal pay in the future.

Hopefully, that equality will be seen in other professional sports, and in salaries in general.

> **"When women thrive, all of society benefits, and succeeding generations are given a better start in life."**
> —Kofi Annan

If we don't demand equal pay, the patriarchy will not give it to us. We're all scared of rejection, but we shouldn't be. What do we have to lose? If we don't ask, it's a "no" anyway! Why shouldn't we be paid for the work we do and for what we're worth? Yes, we're worthy of a fair and livable salary.

Learning to Negotiate

Negotiating for what we want and deserve often holds us back. Ask yourself, "What are others making for the same job?" If you're doing the same work, you deserve the same amount. And don't forget to mention your own experience, strengths, and unique talents. You provide value through your work, and deserve to be paid commensurately in return. And don't forget about benefits! Sometimes the benefits are more important than the exact salary.

If your current position isn't working for you, it's time to leave. Ask yourself, "What does meaningful work look like to me?" What inspires you so much that you lose track of time? Define what you need and want in your life. Who do you need to tell to make it happen? Don't forget to dream big and out loud!

Let's take a look at a few examples of women who were aware of their dream jobs and took the next steps—often with small grants from WOB.

Elena

Elena was taking ESL classes in Houston and working in a nail salon part-time. She came to us for a laptop to help her learn English and become a therapist. She hoped to find a better job so that she could get out of public housing, which was dangerous for her. She wanted to become a stronger woman. She has her laptop now and is using it for English classes and job searches.

Anabella

Anabella is an entrepreneur, starting a holistic health and wellness product line. She dreamed of owning her own store in Las Vegas. We helped her write a business plan, create a budget, buy her domain name, and find a business mentor. Her grant was used to purchase business cards, flyers, and raw materials. She's off and running!

Kate

Kate is a college graduate and hopes to become a teacher. She has two children; the younger is two years old. She knew she had to find more time for herself, to exercise and eat better. She has received a Section 8 Mobile Voucher for housing so she will be able to move her family to a safe place. We helped her with a laptop for school and committed to help her move.

Selena

Selena dreamed of becoming a physician's assistant in Cleveland. She needed help with transportation to her job. She also needed to complete her GED and enroll in beauty school to help her pay for college. She was looking for funding from us to make an emergency move, as her abuser knows where she lives. When she is stable, she wants to bring her son to the US, and is working hard towards that goal. She is learning that she deserves to, and has the power to, change her life one step at a time.

"If you dream little, you get little.
But if you dream big, you get big." —Jo

Invitation to Self-Care and Healing

"Perfection is the enemy." —Sheryl Sandberg

Self-Care: Making the Bed You Want to Lie In

- ✦ Treat yourself as well as you treat your children. This includes supplying yourself with what you need to succeed.
- ✦ Eat a salad: great for your health as well as your wallet! Sing, dance, take a walk. Do something positive for you.
- ✦ Make your bed every morning. It will be waiting for you later.
- ✦ Ask for help at least once this week. It can be for something small, or something large.

What Have I Done Today to Put Me in a Good Position to Succeed Tomorrow?

_____

_____

_____

_____

Affirmations: My Worthiness

- ✦ I am good at what I do.
- ✦ I deserve to be paid fairly for my work.
- ✦ I'm proud of who I'm becoming.
- ✦ I have the power to take the next step I need.
- ✦ I am always learning.

Reasons Why I am Worthy

_____

_____

_____

_____

Journaling: Tools to Negotiate

What does meaningful work look like to me?

_____

_____

_____

_____

How much money do I need to live safely and comfortably?

_____

_____

_____

_____

Could I start out with less money knowing I will get raises over a specific amount of time?

_____

_____

_____

_____

What benefits are most important to me?

_____

_____

_____

_____

Chapter 8

Breaking the Intergenerational Cycle of Intimate Terrorism

CORE BELIEF: Ending abuse saves future generations.

My mother was a smart, beautiful, loving woman who was abused for years by her domineering mother, leaving her open to be abused (and almost killed) by my father. He had suffered from abuse himself, and became a high-functioning alcoholic whose anger was uncontrollable, terrorizing not only my mother, but my brother and me as well.

Intimate terrorism is an *intergenerational epidemic.* I worked with more than 2,200 survivors of intimate terrorism for twelve years, helping them become financially independent and create new lives for themselves and their families. Only then could they save their more than five thousand children from being abused or becoming abusers.

I often heard these incredibly brave women say they had seen their mothers, aunts, grandmothers, sisters, and cousins in abusive relationships. How can anyone know what a healthy relationship is if abuse is all they know growing up? This is also true for abusers; they have either been abused themselves or have seen family members abuse others.

I was lucky that I was too stubborn to become a victim like my mother; I broke the cycle without realizing it. My daughters are smart, loving, independent women and great mothers.

In order to reliably break the cycle, survivors need to recognize and understand their family history and the dynamics that were prevalent. How were the females in the family treated? Was there physical, psychological, or emotional abuse? Were women given a say in the financial matters of the family? Were the children in the family abused in any way? How was anger managed?

Women have to learn how to talk as much as we listen. Men have to learn how to listen as much as they talk."
—Gloria Steinem

Women who have been brought up in abusive families often choose abusers for partners, and men can become abusers after watching abuse in the household because they have not been taught how to handle their own anger. Statistics and studies show us that when "children see that parents use violence in frustrating situations and to cope with difficulty...[they] may be unable to distinguish those instances in which aggression is appropriate and, as a result, develop similar aggressive behavior."[13]

Symptoms of intergenerational trauma include low self-esteem, depression, anxiety, insomnia, anger, and even self-destructive behavior. Survivors of intergenerational intimate terrorism have been trained not to trust themselves, their actions, or their decisions.

What Can Be Done?

As we discussed in Chapter 4, "The Dream Proposal: Dreaming Big and Out Loud," the only real way of breaking this cycle is to leave

13.Finkelhor et. al, The Dark Side of Families; *Current Family Violence Research 1st Edition,* (Sage Publications, 1983).

the abusive relationship and to believe that you don't deserve abuse, even if others in your family were abused.

Often, survivors believe it will be worse for their children and for them if they have to go into a shelter and have no means of support. However, staying with an abuser could become much more dangerous. Many of the women I spoke with had stayed with their abusers way too long because they feared they would not be able to take care of their children outside of the relationship. Often the deciding factor was when the abuser turned their focus to the children. The mothers could not tolerate that.

Knowing when behavior becomes unacceptable is different for each woman. Only then can she make the decision to leave. If you have a friend or relative who is trying to make that decision, don't judge her—just listen and support. Please.

"Black women have had to develop a larger vision of our society than perhaps any other group. They have had to understand white men, white women, and black men. And they have had to understand themselves. When black women win victories, it is a boost for virtually every segment of society." —Angela Davis

How do we break the cycle in the long term? We have to teach children at a very early age that they deserve to be treated with respect and that there is zero tolerance for bullying or mistreating anyone. Mothers, fathers, schools, and athletic teams need to stop the continuation of abuse by teaching very young children that they deserve to be treated with respect and must treat others of all ages and genders with respect. The "boys will be boys" attitude must stop. There needs to be zero tolerance for abuse at home, at work, and in school. Not until abuse and degradation of women is socially unacceptable will the staggering numbers change.

> "I raise up my voice—not so that I can shout but so that those without a voice can be heard...we cannot all succeed when half of us are held back."
> —Malala Yousafzai

We need to learn appropriate outlets for our anger, as anger will always show up when least expected, and should not be denied. We need to listen to our anger and respect where it's coming from. If anger is not given an outlet, it will turn to resentment, which kills relationships and causes other mental and emotional issues. It took me decades to deal with the anger I had toward my father, and it had an impact on my behavior in many different ways, including alcohol use.

Let's hear some stories of brave women who dared to reach out for help and break the intergenerational cycle of trauma in their lives.

Safaya: A Life Too Small

After years of violent abuse, and because she knew her abuser would find her, Safaya was forced to move thousands of miles in order to break her intergenerational cycle of intimate terrorism and save her children. She also had to change her learned attitude of low expectations regarding her goals and personal fulfillment.

Safaya was the first person in her family to go to college. She had never been given any encouragement or support by her family. After her children were born, and while working full time, she felt empty, scared, and totally alone. She wondered if there could be a better, safer life somewhere for she and her children.

She began secretly saving some of her grocery money. Finally, after a year, was able to escape across country with her children. She found a temporary job, which quickly became full-time. Her employers were kind and encouraged her to continue her education.

She is now happily a full-time college student, a full-time employee, and a full-time mother.

Safaya's Dream

Safaya's dream was to pursue higher education and buy a home.

Positive Outcome

She has earned an associate's degree and is working toward her bachelor's. She has a job she loves, she and her children are safe.

Paying It Forward

As a domestic violence victim advocate, Safaya seeks out opportunities to raise awareness of the strength and power of women.

Lesson Learned

Safaya appreciates each positive step she takes. She takes pride in all that she is doing, knowing that it is not only for her, but for her family too.

Juanita

Juanita's dream is to cook for the elderly. She would also like to have a happy family. Her English is limited, and she's taking ESL classes at her domestic violence agency. She has a twelve-year old son whom she loves deeply. One of her requests was for a desk so her son could study. She didn't understand that the grant was for her, not her son.

With a bit of persuasion, Juanita told me that she didn't have a bed for herself. With the housing grant from WOB, she was able to buy a bed that same day. She's also planning to go to college when she finishes her ESL classes.

Katrina

Katrina needed to move to a new, safer apartment. She had two children. They had no beds because of the bedbugs in the place they lived. They also needed new clothes. Katrina's biggest dream was to own a restaurant, and she was taking bartending classes. She admitted that she needed to decrease the stress in her life and get more sleep. We talked about how she might do that.

With our help, Katrina was able to pay the deposit and the first month's rent on her new apartment. We also collaborated with several different agencies to get her furniture and clothing for the whole family. That was the power of reaching out for help.

Anger Management and Recovery from Intergenerational Trauma

I believe anger management can be a meaningful deterrent to intergenerational intimate terrorism. Studies tell us that "the intergenerational transmission of violence approach suggests that children who witness or experience violence learn that violence is appropriate for conflict resolution and is acceptable in intimate interpersonal settings."[14]

14. B. Egeland, "A History of Abuse is a Major Risk Factor for Abusing the Next Generation," in *Current Controversies on Family Violence*, eds. R. J. Gelles and D. R. Loseke (Newbury Park, CA: Sage Publications, 1993).

Like my father, I tried to manage my anger with alcohol; which, of course, had the opposite effect. It was, at the time, the only thing I knew to do. My wonderful family intervened thirty years ago, and I have not had a drink since. I'm one of the lucky ones who didn't need a twelve-step program to quit.

Because of my anger and my alcohol use, I wasn't always the kind of mother that my daughters deserved, so self-forgiveness has been a big part of my journey and recovery.

Learning to Heal

> "The quieter you become,
> the more you can hear." —Ram Dass

Today, there are amazing psychological techniques to help with anger and the other symptoms of trauma from intergenerational intimate terrorism. Cognitive behavioral therapy and dialectical behavior therapy are effective therapies where you don't need to relive your painful past in order to recover.

Cognitive Behavioral Therapy

Cognitive behavioral therapy (CBT) is a common form of "talk therapy." A therapist supports you in becoming conscious of inaccurate or negative thinking. This helps you to understand your situation more clearly and make better decisions about your life and relationships. CBT can help with depression and post-traumatic stress disorder (PTSD).

Dialectical Behavior Therapy

Dialectical behavior therapy (DBT) offers tools to help manage painful emotions as well as stressful relationships more skillfully through mindfulness, assertiveness training, and learning to understand and manage one's negative emotions.

One of my favorite quotations is by Dr. Dan Siegel. He says, "Name it to tame it."[15] Being aware of what you are feeling is the first step in understanding yourself. Then actively labeling the big, scary feelings allows you to have some control over what is happening inside of you. Don't judge yourself: just notice. You are allowed to have whatever thoughts and emotions you have. Know that they will pass. Nobody has the right to tell you that your feelings or thoughts are wrong.

> "Being fully human is not about feeling happy, it's about feeling everything." —Glennon Doyle

Self-Forgiveness

In order to live authentically, we need to take the time to really know ourselves and look within. It's hard, sometimes messy, work. It takes serious self-forgiveness, forgiveness for everything you have imagined that you have ever done wrong. All of our experiences, good and not so good, have gotten us here today. We have always done the best we could do with the tools and knowledge that we had at the time. Our story is our story: unique and deserving to be honored. We're just where we should be to move forward with our dreams.

Here are some reminders to keep close by as you make your way toward your new life free from abuse:

Find support groups. There are survivor groups, single-mom groups, and many others to choose from that can help support you emotionally. The good news is that you will find not only support, but friends there. Support is available in many forms, everywhere. You don't need to do this alone.

15. Dr. Dan J. Siegel and Dr. Tina Payne Bryson, *The Whole-Brain Child*. (New York: Bantam Books, 2012).

Use intention. Concentrate and focus on your desired outcomes and dreams. Commit to achieving your desired goals with baby steps each day. That's really all it takes.

Congratulate yourself. Don't forget to take a moment at the end of the day to acknowledge what you've accomplished. A joyful life cannot be based on fear. Make joy a daily priority—put it in your schedule.

Learn to love your younger self. It took me five years to be able to say, "I love you, little Jo" and mean it. My past had never allowed me to love myself. My mother saying "If you can't say anything nice, don't say anything at all," followed me and played in my head for years. Stop all self-talk unless it's a positive affirmation of how worthy you are. Don't believe any of the stories you tell yourself! Love, self-love, and self-acceptance take practice.

Begin to understand your abuse. Even though this is scary, it can give you huge power. Don't believe self-talk such as "I must be broken." Never fall into the trap of telling yourself, "I can fix this, and I just need to try harder." Doing more and trying harder will never fix what your abuser is doing to you. You cannot change your abuser. Facing this reality is your most important first step to independence.

Be brave. Call out others on inappropriate language or behavior.

Create boundaries and hold people accountable. Practice scripts that you can use in conversations. For example, "That is not appropriate," or "I'll get back to you later on that." Make sure the people you are with share your beliefs. If they do, they will empower and support you.

Strengthen your intuition muscle. Each time you exercise it, it gets stronger. As survivors, our brains have become full of misperceptions, expectations, and assumptions. Instead, make your decisions from your heart and soul. You know they will be the right ones. Notice what your gut is telling you about an idea or a decision. Is the feeling uncomfortable, or is it warm and fuzzy? Trust the feeling.

Be patient. Your recovery will take time. Please find the support that you need. You are who you believe you are. Believe you are wonderful and deserve the best, because you are and you do. Celebrate yourself every day. Living on earth is hard, and being human is hard. Nobody promised it would be easy, but it can still be a dream come true.

Invitation to Self-Care and Healing

"Don't be so humble—you're not that great."
—Golda Meir

Self-Care: How Do I Heal So Others Don't Hurt?

✦ **Take ten breaths between having a feeling and taking action.**

✦ **If you are feeling stuck, get up and move.**

✦ **Drink one more glass of water.**

✦ **Eat one more piece of fruit.**

✦ **Learn a new coping mechanism each month.**

How Have I Cared for Myself to Heal Myself Today?

_____

_____

_____

_____

Affirmations: I Will Not Settle for Less

✦ **I'm worthy of love and respect, and I will not settle for less.**

✦ **I have no expectation of others.**

✦ **I make no assumptions.**

✦ **I trust my inner awareness.**

✦ **The only thing I need to do is my best.**

Reasons I Will Not Settle for Less:

_____

_____

_____

_____

Journaling: Setting Boundaries

How can I voice my anger in a healthy way?

_____

_____

_____

_____

List 3 ways I can be stronger with my boundaries:
1) _____
2) _____
3) _____

What can I say or do to avoid uncomfortable situations?

_____

_____

_____

_____

What beliefs from growing up hold me back?

_____

_____

_____

_____

How can I use my new beliefs today?

_____

_____

_____

_____

Chapter 9

Paying It Forward: Our Superpower

———

CORE BELIEF: "Paying it forward" through good works exponentially helps other women and increases an individual's feeling of self-worth. Giving to others is empowering.

I didn't know it at the time, but while driving home from the shelter in 2003 after I had given $40 to help a survivor and her family, I began the most important "pay it forward" of my life. It lasted more than twelve years. I worked tirelessly without pay and was often exhausted, frustrated, and discouraged, but I gained more personally than I ever gave.

My journey all started with the knowledge that this was something I was meant to do. The choice was not well-thought-out or planned. The dream came later, when I decided how to create Web of Benefit.

I put together a board of directors made up of savvy, committed women to help with my vision to give grants to one hundred survivors of intimate terrorism. I hoped to raise $100,000 to give grants of $1,000 each.

I had to research how to run a board meeting, as the IRS required four meetings a year to maintain our nonprofit status. All this was very intimidating to me. I needed to do it right, or WOB would lose its nonprofit classification; my fundraising would be over, as gifts would no longer be tax deductible, and no foundation or corporation would touch us.

At our first meeting, two ideas were brought up: one by a wealthy friend, who was the most knowledgeable of us about nonprofits, and one by my younger daughter. The first idea was that we hire a director of development to do all the fundraising. This, of course, was impossible, as we had no funds to pay for anyone. The second idea, from my daughter, became one of the founding principles of the organization—our Good Works Agreement, or a way to "pay it forward."

The Good Works Agreement

The movie *Pay It Forward* had recently come out, and it'd had an impact on my daughter and me. It was based on the belief that if people would do three good deeds to pay back one good deed done for them, this could change the world. My daughter suggested that if each of our grantees would commit to paying it forward to three other women, this would exponentially increase our influence, even though our funds were so limited.

Our "Good Works Agreement" was created to put that commitment into writing. Each grant recipient had to sign the agreement below.

Good Works Agreement

Because Web of Benefit was created by women for the purpose of empowering women, I agree to increase this web by helping three other women who have survived domestic violence, in whatever fashion I'm able, without expectation of repayment. This might include babysitting, cooking, driving, advising other women on job or educational opportunities, mentoring, or even referring a woman to Web of Benefit, Inc.

I also agree to provide feedback to Web of Benefit, Inc. by completing an online survey describing my progress in reaching my personal goals and also the help I have given to other survivors after one year.

Signed by:

Date:

Paying it forward became a way for WOB to create a network of trust and a sense of community in which women could feel safe. It also helped to give others who we couldn't assist directly the support they needed to achieve independence and reach their highest potential. They were practicing gratitude in their new lives.

Our grantees paid it forward more than ten thousand times, doing small favors to help others for years; some even made it their future profession.

Here are just a few of the many ways these 2,200 women went on to pay it forward and, by doing so, participate in helping to end the cycle of intimate terrorism for other women.

Barbara's Story: The Ring

Barbara sold what had once been one of her prized possessions, her wedding ring, to help another survivor so that her dreams might come true. This is what pay it forward is all about. At the time Barbara wrote this for us, she had been divorced and was happily remarried with a new ring.

In Her Own Words

" I was all ready for the wedding—just had to slip the gown over my head. Instead, I lay face down on the floor and cried. "All brides are nervous," my friend said, patting my back. No, this was worse. I knew not to go through with it, but I didn't trust my inner voice. Plus, all the guests were waiting...

I cried again every time he belittled me, when he cheated, when he shoved me, when he broke my ribs. I cried the day I took off my wedding ring—it was our fifteenth anniversary—and he didn't even notice. I put the ring into my sock drawer. I didn't want to look at it. I couldn't imagine that my daughter would want the symbol of such an unhappy union. I almost threw it into a nearby river but feared that a fisherman would find it, identify me by the engraving, and return it. I didn't know what to do with it.

That ring stayed in the sock drawer for twenty more years—until I heard that Web of Benefit had a program in which the ring could be sold and the proceeds used to help another woman start a new life after abuse.

I cried when I wrapped up that ring and mailed it in. I thought of the ancient alchemists who attempted to transform base medals into gold. "May this gold ring be transformed into something higher," I wished. Here's to your dreams, my sisters! **"**

"Alone we can do so little; together we can do
so much." —Helen Keller

Dr. Kay's Story: A PhD

I met Dr. Kay while working with another agency in Boston. I knew when I met her that she was someone I wanted to get to know better. Her determination and commitment were wonderful to see. We became friends, and she joined our board and ultimately became our president. She has never stopped paying it forward.

In Her Own Words

" My name is Dr. Kay, and I'm a survivor of domestic violence. After moving to Massachusetts, I began to think about what my dreams were as a child and what I wanted to be when I grew up. I recall my mother and family members wanting me to be a lawyer; that was not my dream. I went back to school after thirty-two years and received my master's degree in business and graduated from Cambridge College in 2003. After carefully considering my options, I decided I wanted to pursue a doctoral degree in business administration. Four years later, I went to an organization for assistance because I wanted to complete my education. The woman there told me about Web of Benefit and that a woman would be in her office the next week. She advised me to come back then because the organization couldn't help me with a grant, but WOB could.

I went back the next week and met Jo. She asked me about my "BIG" dream and I filled out the questionnaire. I told her about wanting a doctoral degree in business administration. I had already registered but couldn't afford to begin. Jo made my dream come to life by providing me with a grant to fund my first semester in the doctoral program at the

University of Phoenix. A few years later, I graduated with my doctorate in business administration.

A few years after that, I was asked to be the president of Web of Benefit, which was truly an honor, and it allowed me the opportunity to see the program in action as we aided other women in fulfilling their dreams.

Because of the support I received from the organization, I've been paying it forward every day. I work with women of all ethnicities and assist them in any way I can, freely.

Because I believed that anything was possible and prayed long and hard about the next step in my life, God put people in my life who believed in me and wanted to help me fulfill my dreams. Thanks to WOB and Jo for all the love and support over the years.

Web of Benefit changed my life and my outlook on life as well. Today, I know that lost dreams can come true, too! My husband (Thaddeus), our dog (Ghost), and I are truly grateful that such a program was available to me and so many others. 𝟫𝟫

"Giving liberates the soul of the giver."
—Maya Angelou

What I didn't know at the time I started my outreach to other abused women is that being able to help someone else, even in a small way, is the most empowering thing in the world. My own "pay it forward" changed my life in ways I never could have imagined. It gave me purpose and satisfaction that I never dreamed possible. I learned

I was worthy to have my biggest dream come true. Giving to others is a superpower, and it empowers at the same time.

The following three survivors describe how their lives have been transformed by their superpower of paying it forward.

Mariko

Since her interview and being granted a computer, Mariko had been very motivated. She completed the forty-hour domestic violence volunteer training and started volunteering at a shelter as her way to pay it forward. She also completed her certification as an alcohol and drug counselor. She believed that would be a perfect job for her.

Irene

Irene now shares her experiences of sexual abuse, exploitation, and racism with other survivors. She writes: "Knowing that I survived these traumas wasn't enough for me; I needed to do something that would help me accept these experiences on a different level, and paying it forward has filled that void. It shifts my perspective from self-centered to help-centered, allowing me to move from a survivor to a helper."

Adriana

Adriana had been helping homeless and hungry people with pocket change, but wanted to do more. She believes all people deserve to have a voice and to live in safe housing. She is researching how to start her own nonprofit to help the homeless.

"There's no greater gift than thinking that you had some impact on the world, for the better." —Gloria Steinem

Jo's Earned Wisdom

For many decades I was on autopilot, focusing on what I was "supposed to:" kids, husband, home, job, etc. Creating Web of Benefit forced me to do some serious soul-searching—it was probably time at age fifty-seven! I needed to understand what I believed to be most important in my life before I could do anything else. Call it an overdue midlife crisis. I discovered the following:

- I believe in honesty, integrity, transparency, and accountability.

- I believe that one woman can make a difference, and women working together can change the world through a "web of benefit."

- I believe that all women deserve to live free of violence and to create the lives of their dreams.

- I believe that domestic violence is an intergenerational cycle that can be broken only by empowering survivors to become self-sufficient and financially independent with the ongoing support of multiple collaborating organizations.

- I believe all women need to create a network of trust to support one another.

- I believe that worthiness is the foundation of women's power. If a woman truly believes that she deserves to have her dreams become reality, she has the power to create them.

- I believe women need to dream big and focus small. A unique life vision needs to be created by each individual, with specific steps and goals defined.

- I believe the "pay it forward" philosophy exponentially increases the "web of benefit," and also empowers women by reminding them they have the ability to help someone else.

"We know that when a woman speaks truth to power, there will be attempts to put her down...I'm not going to go anywhere. —Maxine Waters

My final wish is that you will realize your greatest power comes from helping others. I hope that you find joy in "paying it forward" to others daily, in small and not-so-small ways. I believe real power comes from the desire and ability to empower others. Paying it forward will come back to you in ways you cannot imagine.

Invitation to Self-Care and Healing

"Don't look for big things, just do small things with great love." —Mother Teresa

Self-Care: Practice Paying It Forward with Baby Steps

✦ **Pay it forward at least once today. It will feel great:**

- **Smile at a stranger.**
- **Hold the door.**
- **Thank someone.**
- **Send love to a stranger.**
- **Listen to someone.**
- **Call a friend.**
- **Ask someone if you can help them.**

✦ **Trust your boundaries. Help others when you can, but don't feel guilty when you can't. Say "no" just for practice!**

What Have I Done to Pay It Forward Today?

_____

_____

_____

_____

Affirmations: Abundance

✦ **I believe in abundance.**

✦ **The friends/support I need are out there.**

- ✦ **I'm perfect just as I am.**
- ✦ **I believe in magic.**
- ✦ **I verbalize my anger in healthy ways.**

My Abundant Affirmations:

_____

_____

_____

_____

Journaling: Compassion for Others

How did I make a difference today?

_____

_____

_____

_____

List 3 people I helped this week:

1) _____
2) _____
3) _____

What was one moment of joy today?

_____

_____

_____

_____

What is my special gift?

_____

_____

_____

_____

What am I grateful to have received from others?

_____

_____

_____

_____

Chapter 10

Empowered Women Working Together to Change the World

"Behind every great woman...is another great woman."
—Kate Hodges

CORE BELIEF: One woman can make a difference. Women working together can change the world.

The core belief of this chapter became a founding philosophy of Web of Benefit. Because "synergy" is one of my favorite words, and because I believe in "the whole is greater than the sum of its parts" idea that one plus one equals three, I knew from the beginning that I could not do what I wanted to do alone.

The name "Web of Benefit" came from my vision of a group of women collaborating to help other women. I needed to create interconnected groups of women with the mission of helping survivors define and achieve their dreams for better lives.

One of our pro-bono nonprofit consultants spent months trying to figure out better fundraising and organizational strategies for us, and finally came up with the idea that I should change our name. I was surprised and, honestly, a bit hurt that they thought that was an option. I asked why, and the answer was that, "It reminds people of a spider web!" That was exactly what it was supposed to do!

Two years later, the man(!) who came up with that idea apologized to me, saying he realized this wasn't a smart idea.

The collaboration I created consisted of a board of directors made up totally of women. We had women volunteers and interns; hundreds of women donors; more than 250 women advocates from domestic violence agencies; women from collaborating agencies, foundations, and corporations; and women consultants.

Full disclosure: In later years, we had a wonderful young man who had been one of my first interns from Babson College, my alma mater, join our board. He was very brave to become the only male in an all-female organization. Thank you, Sean!

Over the years, I observed tireless domestic violence advocates working one-on-one with survivors to give help and support; each one made a huge difference in their clients' individual lives. I also saw that they did not have the funding to help in meaningful, economic ways. All these agencies have very limited funding, with nothing to give to survivors in any flexible way. I knew we all needed to work together to begin to create new lives. This truly was synergy at its best.

> "I can promise you that women working together—linked, informed and educated—can bring peace and prosperity to this forsaken planet."
> —Isabel Allende

When I was organizing WOB and trying to understand fundraising, I decided that we would not take any public or government money from anywhere. This decision probably wasn't smart from a fundraising perspective, but it turned out to be the most important decision in making us unique within the country. When a domestic violence agency accepts public funding, there are huge strings attached when it comes to reporting procedures—but most importantly, the funds need to be spent in the state where they were given. Our uniqueness came from our ability to give grants *immediately*, often on an emergency basis, in twenty-six states by Skype (long before Zoom existed).

For example, a domestic violence advocate, who later became a board member, called me one morning at 9:00 a.m. with an emergency that needed immediate attention; she knew there was no other organization that could help in time.

A survivor had already moved into her new apartment because she had been promised funding for the security deposit by another agency. After years of being separated from them, she finally had her children back with her. That morning, she learned that the promised government funds were not coming. She needed to pay the landlord by 5:00 p.m. or be kicked out of her apartment, and her children would be put back into foster care.

I cancelled my appointments and got there by noon. We completed her application and Dream Proposal, and when the interview was over, WOB wrote the check, and the woman delivered it to her landlord by 5:00 p.m.

Women and Nonprofits

According to networkforgood.com, only 21 percent of nonprofit organizations in the United States are run by women, and those women make only 66 percent of the salaries earned by men.

I'm including some of my favorite women-run organizations, created to empower women and girls, that are changing the world. It is my hope that you might look at these organizations and find one that interests you, or find others that you might love and become involved with in some small way. They appear in no specific order of priority.

Favorite Women-Run Organizations

Girls Who Code (www.girlswhocode.com) educates middle and high school girls with the mission of "gender parity in computer science by 2027." Its founder is Reshma Saujani. When asked about her professional mission, she said, "Fail fast, fail hard, fail often. Failure is the key to success."

She Should Run (www.sheshouldrun.org) has the mission to "inspire the next generation of women to run for government office in the US." Its founder is Erin Loos Cutraro. Since 2011, the organization has encouraged 30,000 women to run for office at all levels.

One Love Foundation (www.joinonelove.org) has the mission to educate all people about what healthy relationships should look like. Katie Hood is the CEO. The organization has 44,000 volunteers, and 1.6 million individuals have attended their workshops.

Women For Women International (www.womenforwomen.org) was founded by Zainab Salbi. She says, "The single thing all women need in the world is inspiration, and inspiration comes from storytelling." She created a one-year program to help women survivors of war become financially independent. They have helped more than 478,000 women in eight countries.

The Malala Fund (www.malala.org) was founded by Malala Yousafzai. Its mission is to educate women and children around the world.

"When unique voices are united in a common cause, they make history." —Gloria Steinem

It is my belief that all good things start from the bottom up, not from the top down. Brave individuals with vision and passion create our best organizations and corporations. Entrepreneurs, especially women entrepreneurs, are the lifeblood of our country. Many of the women who were helped by small grants from WOB went on to change their lives significantly as a result of the (minimal) financial help coupled with strong emotional support from WOB, advocates, social services, and other women paying it forward.

Testimonials

The testimonials below from recipients, advocates, and donors not only illustrate what one woman's dream can create, but also the power of women working together.

"Often, I have thought what a benefit it would be to a certain client 'if only' we had the funds to provide a laptop to support an educational goal or employment opportunity. Web of Benefit has been the solution to many of my 'if only' dilemmas this year. Thank you." —Advocate

"What makes Web of Benefit one of a kind is its ability not only to give a grant in less than 24 hours in case of emergencies, but also to design an award to meet a woman's specific needs to help her with the first step toward her dream. This flexibility and efficiency are possible because WOB does not take government or public funding." —Collaborating Agency

"You helped us at a time that we were in much need of help and didn't know where to turn. It was very helpful not only financially, but spiritually. It is amazing that an organization like yours exists, because we were starting to lose faith that we would be able to receive help at all. There aren't enough words to describe how grateful we are to you." —Daughter of Grantee

"I don't think you understand quite what you did for me. I had emailed or called every resource I could find from the federal level down. Your organization is the single source that actually helped me in a tangible way when I was desperate and would not have had any funds to pay my mortgage or keep my slim grip on sanity. Blessings to you." —Grantee

"We still can't imagine how you do so much with so little, but we're proud and happy to have a part in it. And that you aren't stopping there is great. In the 25+ years I have spent with the foundation, I have never known any group to help so many, and so personally and so effectively, with so little. Please keep us in mind for the future, because we hope you aren't done yet." —Loyal Funder

"Thank you for all you have done for women who needed a hand up and not a handout. WOB, you have been part of my empowerment success for six years, through twenty-seven grateful women, twenty-three laptops, four tuition enrollments, and even a down payment on a car. You have assisted women in following their dreams, which have come true for several women, such as getting a degree, starting a business or working at a medical facility, purchasing a car, buying a condo, etc."

"WOB also helped me with my dreams. Although we never spoke about it, I, too, am a survivor, and you helped me for the last few years to not only become aware of how significant I am, but how I've made a difference in so many others' lives. You have truly been a blessing to hundreds of people, because when you touch one, that one touches others." —Advocate

Invitation to Self-Care and Healing

"Make the most of yourself by fanning the tiny, inner sparks of possibility into flames of achievement."
—Golda Meir

Self-Care: Empowering Yourself

✦ Look in the mirror and say "Hello, wonderful!" You are beautiful just as you are.

✦ Pick a group: friends, family, coworkers, community, or women's organization. Find one new person to support you from that group. Do the same next week!

✦ Give yourself an extra half-hour of sleep to better face the next day.

✦ Play quiet music, play loud music.

✦ Sit in the sun, and wear sunblock.

What Have I Done to Empower Myself Today?

_____

_____

_____

_____

Affirmations: I Am Empowered

✦ I allow joy to happen because I deserve it.

✦ I'm proud of my unique beauty, inside and outside.

✦ I'm learning about myself every day.

✦ **I embrace all parts of myself.**

✦ **I am capable of doing difficult things**

My Empowering Affirmations:

_____

_____

_____

_____

Journaling: What can you do for yourself?

List 2 past mistakes:

1) _____

2) _____

How can I forgive myself for them?

1) _____

2) _____

What do I want today?

_____

_____

_____

_____

What did I do that I am proud of today?

_____

_____

_____

_____

Jo Crawford

What 3 good things can I do for the world?
1) _____
2) _____
3) _____

How do I want to help?

_____
_____
_____
_____

Chapter 11

Creating and Recreating Your Dreams at Any Age

CORE BELIEF: You are never too old to create your dream.

As I sit to write the last chapter of my one and only book, I'm incredibly grateful to be a healthy, active, seventy-six-year-old woman. God has been good to me in every way, even in the not-so-good times.

Gail Sheehy wrote her wonderful book *Sex and the Seasoned Woman* when she was seventy years old. She said a "seasoned woman" is "marinated in life experience" and "knows who she is." She also believes that if a woman reaches the age of fifty without cancer or heart disease, she can expect to live to be ninety-two.

Sheehy speaks of two adulthoods—the first is from age thirty to age fifty, and the second is from age fifty to age ninety. If we believe this to be true, we wouldn't retire at age sixty or sixty-five; we'd be planning for the next twenty-five or thirty years with a whole new dream.

Mary Pipher wrote her book *Women Rowing North* at age seventy-two. She says "happiness is a choice and a set of skills," and "the way we think about aging can actually impact our DNA, as well as many other aspects of our later years." She believes that the way we handle our lives involves "attitude and coping capacities."

> "It's not how old you are, it's how you are old."
> —Jules Renard

I was fifty-seven years old before I had a clue what I was going to do when I grew up. Better late than never! How often the biggest and best things in our lives seem to happen by mistake. I have come to believe that there really are no mistakes: that the universe is creating magic for us.

Rose's Story: As Simple as Closing My Eyes

I had the honor of reconnecting with Rose in early 2022. She's happily married, owns her own home, and has a wonderful new job. Her son is doing well in eighth grade. Having come from a Muslim country, her ability to remember her innate power has changed her life in ways she never could have imagined.

In Her Own Words

❝ *Lost and confused were my emotional feelings when I first met Jo at the domestic violence shelter. At that time, I didn't know what her connection to the shelter was or how she could be helping someone like me who was traumatized, scared, and spoke only a few words of English.*

At first, Jo handed me the Dream Proposal and asked me to close my eyes and think about my aspirations and my future dreams. I thought to myself that this woman couldn't be serious because I was living a nightmare that repeated itself daily as I was going through a divorce. I had no roof over my head and a baby in my arms. It wasn't as simple as closing my eyes! I relaxed a bit when she started talking about how the program helped many women live their dreams. I listened but understood only half of what was said to me. I had to focus hard to write down what I wanted to be in the future. After a little while, I finally handed Jo a piece of paper that said "I would like to become a graphic designer."

Jo took the piece of paper, folded it, and hid it in her notebook. Then she asked me about immediate needs that could lead me to accomplish this dream. Still confused and with my limited vocabulary, I mentioned to her that I had to take English classes and needed a replacement of my green card, which had been confiscated by my ex-husband.

In my entire interaction with Jo that day, I was amazed at how sensitive and compassionate she was about my situation and how hard she tried to make sense of our communication. Soon after our conversation, I got a check for the amount of $375 to get a replacement for my green card. I registered for English classes with the help of the shelter and started getting monthly transportation passes for more than a year because after I finished ESL classes, I trained as an intern at a financial institution in the marketing department. This path led me to pursuing my dream at a community college. It took me two years to get my associate's degree in graphic design, and I kept that motivation to transfer to a four-year school where I earned a bachelor's degree in business marketing and later on an MBA in international business.

I really didn't know how I accomplished all that while I had a limited belief in myself at that time. I believed that my past circumstances held me captive, but in reality, the school helped me heal. I probably didn't get there the same way other regular students did, but I always remembered Jo's advice at our first meeting: "Dreams come true if you focus on accomplishing small steps." Jo's voice followed me whenever I tried to give up and told myself that my dream wasn't doable. Jo checked on me throughout the years to make sure I was still following through. Each email I got from her told me to "dream big" or to dream even bigger.

I do believe that dreams don't have a deadline; this is why I'm chasing a different kind of dream right now, which is finding my dream job. I would really be happy if my next position is in integrated marketing communications at an international company where I can utilize my graphic design and marketing skills. **"**

Rose's Dream

Rose's dream had multiple steps, which she took one at a time: learn English, replace her green card, get an apartment, earn a college degree, and become a graphic designer.

Positive Outcome

Rose became a US citizen, received an MBA, got married, bought a house, and has a happy and healthy son in eighth grade.

Paying It Forward

Rose was able to help the shelter right away with graphic design as well as help other women at the shelter by babysitting and teaching them how to use a computer.

Lesson Learned

Rose learned that dreams don't have a deadline.

Heroines have continued to do extraordinary work for decades, creating new dreams as they go. With the wisdom of age, we're able to see the bigger picture of what the world needs and live fearlessly. Failure is no longer even a consideration.

AARP Purpose Prize

Every year, the American Association of Retired Persons honors exceptional women (and men) with the Purpose Prize, which recognizes individuals aged fifty and older who "have dedicated their lives to serving others in creative and innovative ways." CEO Jo Ann Jenkins stated, "During these trying times in our country and globally, we are inspired to see people use their life experiences to build a better future for us all." Below are two heroines who have continued to do extraordinary work for decades.

Cynthia Barnett

Cynthia was seventy-four years old when she founded Amazing Girls Science (www.amazinggirlsscience.com). More than five hundred young women participate annually in Amazing Girls programs, including fifteen educational programs, camps, and classes in computer science, robotics, and coding.

Rita Zimmer

Rita began her nonprofit work in 1983 by creating Women in Need, an organization for homeless women. In 2011, she founded HousingPlus (housingplusnyc.org) in order to provide "community-based housing and comprehensive services to women—including women with children—to support them in overcoming poverty, homelessness, addiction, trauma, and the effects of incarceration."

> "In the future, there will be no female
> leaders. There will just be leaders."
> —Sheryl Sandberg

But women don't have to win awards to be noticed for their extraordinary gifts and achievements. Here are some good examples.

Cecile Richards

Cecile co-founded The Supermajority (supermajority.com) at age sixty-two after retiring as CEO of Planned Parenthood. It is "a multiracial coalition of women" with the mission of "building women's power across the country by training and mobilizing a multiracial intergenerational community who will lead the fight for gender equality." She's been politically active since she was a teenager, and has no plans of stopping.

Marie Yovanovitch

In October of 2019, I had the privilege of watching Marie Yovanovitch, a thirty-year veteran of foreign service and then-recently recalled ambassador to Ukraine, walk proudly across Capitol grounds to give testimony in President Trump's first impeachment hearing. She is the personification of the empowerment I wish for all women worldwide. She defied the pressure from the White House and her boss, Former Secretary of State Mike Pompeo. Her life and her job were at risk, but she stood up against male power and proved that a woman, all women, can walk through fear to stand up for themselves and their country. At age sixty-four, she's a hero, a patriot, and an example of what all women can be.

"Each time a woman stands up for herself,
without knowing it possibly, without claiming it,
she stands up for all women." —Maya Angelou

Irene

Irene is an advocate whom I often collaborated with in Boston. She's also a grant recipient. She writes:

"No, I'm never too old to create and realize my dream. For many years, I dreamed of obtaining my degree. In my younger years, I received a full scholarship to college, and was not able to attend as the result of substance use, exploitation, and domestic violence. However, three years ago I was given a second chance when I received a second full scholarship. In May 2019, at the tender age of sixty, I obtained my degree. Although I'm a little older, I was ecstatic when I was handed my degree. I'm currently completing the necessary paperwork to obtain a master's degree in social work. It's never, ever too late to create and realize your dreams."

Perspective

For me to say that with time and experience comes perspective is an oversimplified cliché. We use words so frequently that we often don't define their unique meaning to us personally. What is your truth? What is perspective? What is love? What is a relationship? If you don't know what these words mean to you, how can you identify your wants and your needs?

"The most important thing is to actually think about
what you do." —Jane Goodall

I believe perspective is knowing that any situation that looks and feels terrible in this moment may not be so horrible in a week, a month, a year, or even five years. Look back on a debilitating situation in your life. How does it feel now? Did it lead you to a better place, a better understanding, a stronger sense of self? Sometimes what was dreadful at the time can become a positive thing in the big picture of your life. Consider: what lesson did it teach you? Did it force you to change something in your life for the better?

> **"There are only two ways to live your life. One is as though nothing is a miracle. The other is as though everything is a miracle." —Albert Einstein**

For me, it took a long time to define "love" in a meaningful way. I believe love is cherishing the good and the bad in our loved ones, knowing we're all imperfect beings just trying to find our way and learn our lessons. For me, love is supporting others in their dreams and helping them to become the best they can be. Love is a verb. It demands action and hard work.

Considering Relationships

What does it mean to be in a relationship? How often do women think of themselves first? You may be saying to yourself, "I can't do that: that's selfish." It *isn't* selfish. You *do* come first. What is your relationship with yourself? That is the most important one.

What do you want and need in a relationship, any relationship? I need honesty, integrity, open communication, caring, compassion, humor, and fun. You get to decide—only you. That's where boundaries come in. One of my favorite quotes is: "'No' is a complete sentence." We never have to justify our thoughts, emotions, or needs.

We often, incorrectly, assume people define these things the same way we do. That is the tragedy of assumptions.

I knew very little about any of this when I started Web of Benefit. What I did have was my vision, my passion, my good intuition, my lack of fear, and my personal need to do something, no matter how small, to end the intergenerational cycle of intimate terrorism.

> "Fake it till you make it. Confidence is so key to women's leadership, we must embrace risk in order to break barriers." —Reshma Saujani

I've thought a lot about what to say to women who want to make a difference in the world and hardly know how to start, yet am compelled to offer my thoughts. I hope that some of my ideas might help you. I do believe that one woman can make a difference, and women working together can change the world.

Ask yourself these questions: What is your vision for the world change that you want? What does your big picture of success look like? What are your dreams and passions? The bottom line is that you must believe you deserve it and that you have the power to create it.

When you start planning your new venture, whatever it might be, I advise you to dream big, focus small, define your mission very simply, and *have no fear*. There is no downside other than not trying at all.

Gloria Steinem so wisely said, "I'm beginning to realize the pleasure of being a nothing-to-lose, take-no-shit, older woman." I fully agree! I don't and never will have all the answers to my life's questions, but I'll never stop learning from each hardship. Change is scary, but being stuck is scarier. I can move. I can learn. I can be grateful, starting with the very smallest gifts.

You can define your beliefs any way you want. They're yours alone. That's scary, but empowering. You can be exactly who you want to be, but that makes who you are your responsibility alone.

By being authentic, you feed who you are. Trust the future to take care of itself. Dare to be different. You're not a victim, you're a survivor!

Self-Care for the Road: Practice Inner Fitness

Tara Parker-Pope tells us, "Inner fitness means focusing your energy on your emotional well-being and mental health rather than berating yourself about your diet, weight, or not getting enough exercise."[16] Practice inner fitness every day.

Self-Care: Inner Fitness Strategies

✦ **Take a long bath.**

✦ **Remember you did something well today.**

✦ **Relax with breathing. Inhale slowly to the count of five, hold to the count of two, and exhale slowly to the count of seven.**

✦ **Repeat three times.**

✦ **Find one person you can talk to.**

✦ **Turn the clock in your bedroom away from you.**

How Have I Practiced Inner Fitness Today?

_____

_____

_____

_____

16. Tara Parker-Pope, "For Better Health, Try Fitness From the Inside Out," *The New York Times*, March 31, 2022.

Affirmations: I'm Extraordinary at Every Age

- ✦ **My attitude can change my life.**
- ✦ **I can verbalize my needs.**
- ✦ **Worrying does not help me.**
- ✦ **I hold my head up.**
- ✦ **I am aging positively.**

Some Affirmations for Me at Every Age:

_____

_____

_____

_____

Journaling: My Ideal Older Self

Why does my story matter?

_____

_____

_____

_____

What does self-compassion mean to me?

_____

_____

_____

_____

What kind of older woman do I want to be?

_____

_____

_____

_____

Jo Crawford

What are five things I'm grateful for?

1) _____

2) _____

3) _____

4) _____

5) _____

How does my future self feel about me?

_____

_____

_____

_____

Am I being true to the person I want to become?

_____

_____

_____

_____

A Message from Jo to Take with You

"It took me quite a long time to develop a voice,
and now that I have it, I am not going to be silent."
—Madeleine Albright

Now that our journey together is coming to a close, I want to leave you with some ideas, reminders, and takeaways that I hope that you've absorbed from my writing and from the stories of so many extraordinary survivors.

We, as women, still have many uphill battles to fight. Patriarchy, sexism, and ageism are all systemic. For non-white women, add racism on top of everything else. There is continued, blatant pay discrimination. We're expected to "behave" from a very early age. As Alexandria Ocasio-Cortez says, "They'll tell you you're too loud, that you need to wait your turn and ask the right people for permission. Do it anyway."

The good news is that the latest census shows we're becoming a non-white country. At the same time, many white men panic about losing power, and make voter suppression and taking away women's rights their top priority.

Time is on our side. We will prevail. But in the meantime, we suffer small and large abuses every day. Not only do we need to believe that we deserve the best and are certainly equal to men in every way, but we also need to have the courage to demonstrate our beliefs, to vote, to run for office, and to just take up more space as we loudly voice our needs and those of our less-fortunate sisters. We're the "supermajority," and we need to own it. Here's how Coretta Scott King said it: "Women, if the soul of the nation is to be saved, I believe that you must become its soul."

Here are a few of the key points we've contemplated in our journey together:

- Women already have all the power we will ever need. They need only to remember and own that power.

- Worthiness is a birthright stolen from us by years of patriarchy and abuse.

- Honor your thoughts and emotions. Nobody can take them away from you. Take the time to put words to them; this takes their negative power away.

- Anger warns us that something needs to change. It may save your life.

- Practicing gratitude for even the smallest thing in our lives creates optimism and hope.

The one sure thing in life is change. Let change become your opportunity to move forward.

Let your dreams become the roadmap for the rest of your life. Dream big and out loud! With creative intentions, you will thrive. You can find new passion at any age. Start with just one baby step; the rest will take care of itself.

- Imagine success, action, goals, first steps. Don't miss anything because of fear.

- Figure out what you need in order to start.

- Find those in your life who will support you.

- Self-care starts with self-compassion, self-forgiveness, and self-love. Remember the neglected, most loveable child within you.

- Forget perfection. Be proud of who you already are. Glennon Doyle admits, "I'm a hot mess and proud of it."

- Treat yourself the way you treat your best friend. Be your own best friend.

- Practices such as journaling, meditation, nutrition, gratitude, affirmations, yoga, and exercise make a huge difference.

- Know and stick to your boundaries. Look for red flags in any relationship. People show you who they are quickly if you look for the signs.

- Always put yourself first.

- Pay it forward. Help others—it's empowering.

When I write about paying it forward, I also mean any form of philanthropy. The definition that I like is "the effort to increase the well-being of humankind as by charitable acts or donations." I believe philanthropy should be a way of being, a verb. We often think of Bill Gates or Warren Buffett, but I also think of my granddaughter who, by the age of eleven, had already grown and cut her long hair twice to donate towards wigs for children with cancer. Philanthropy can be practiced in very small ways with huge effect.

In closing, my prayer for you is that you feel no guilt, no shame, and take no blame for your abuse. You never deserve any form of abuse. Remember: abuse is never about what you have done or who you are. It's always about who and what your abuser really is.

Always trust your intuition. Help is there for you, no matter where in your process you are.

We don't have to be victims; we can be survivors.

We all deserve our best lives simply because we exist.

We all have the power to create the life of our dreams.

We are never alone.

A Call to Action

If you have read this book, you have learned that a very small amount of money put toward a specific need or dream can change a woman's life in huge ways. I have pledged that every penny that this book earns will go to women and their dreams.

Please consider looking for individual women, whom you might see in your everyday life, who would benefit from a small amount to help with their goals and dreams. Perhaps save enough so you could give $300 or $500 for them to take a specific step. You will change a life, and probably a family.

Thank you.

> "Great acts are made up of small deeds."
> —Lao-tzu

Suggested Reading

———

Codependent No More, Melody Beattie

From Strength to Strength, Arthur Brooks

The Gifts of Imperfection, Brené Brown

Welcoming the Unwelcome, Pema Chodron

Untamed, Glennon Doyle

The Power of Intention, Wayne Dyer

The Dark Side of the Light Chasers, Debbie Ford

Empowering Women, Louise Hay

The Power Is Within You, Louise Hay

How to See Yourself as You Really Are, His Holiness the Dalai Lama

Wherever You Go, There You Are, Jon Kabat-Zinn

The Dance of Anger, Harriet Lerner

The Dance of Connection, Harriet Lerner

Fish, Steven Lundin

Anatomy of the Spirit, Caroline Myss

All books, Kristin Neff

The Book You Were Born to Write, Kelly Notaras

Women Rowing North, Mary Pipher

The Little Book of Letting Go, Hugh Prather

The Four Agreements, Don Miguel Ruiz

The Mindful Brain, Dan Siegel

Sex and the Seasoned Woman, Gail Sheehy

Trauma-Informed Yoga, Joanne Spence

Healing from Hidden Abuse, Shannon Thomas

Resources

———

Domestic Violence Information

Domestic violence statistics | National Domestic Violence Hotline
https://www.ncadv.org/statistics

Dynamics of Abuse | National Domestic Violence Hotline
https://www.ncadv.org/dynamics-of-abuse

Signs of Abuse | National Domestic Violence Hotline
https://https://www.ncadv.org/signs-of-abuse

Types of abuse
https://www.womenagainstabuse.org/education-resources/learn-about-abuse/types-of-domestic-violence

What is Gaslighting?
https://www.verywellmind.com/is-someone-gaslighting-you-4147470

Domestic Violence Survivors

These resources provide guidance on national resources available, as well as how to locate state-based services. Although I could not list services for all 52 states, please know that state-based services exist and can be found by exploring the links below and through independent research.

Domestic Shelters
https: /www.domesticshelters.org/domestic-violence-sexual-assault-state-coalitions

Domestic Violence Resources by State
https://www.findlaw.com/family/domestic-violence/domestic-violence-information-by-state.html

Her Voice
https://www.her-voice.net/mentorship

Joyful Heart Foundation
https://www.joyfulheartfoundation.org/

Live Your Dream Resources
https://www.liveyourdream.org/get-help/domestic-violence-resources.html

Love is Respect
https://www.loveisrespect.org/

My Plan App
https://myplanapp.org/

Office of Victims of Crime
https://ovc.ojp.gov/help-for-victims/help-in-your-state

National Coalition Against Domestic Violence (each state has its own) https://www.ncadv.org/resources

National Center on Domestic Violence Trauma, and Mental Health
https://www.nationalcenterdvtraumamh.org/resources/national-domestic-violence-organizations

National Domestic Violence Hotline
https://https://www.thehotline.org

National Network to End Domestic Violence
http://www.nnedv.org

StrongHearts Native Helpline
https://www.strongheartshelpline.org/

YWCA
https://www.ywca.org

Create an Escape Plan | National Domestic Violence Hotline
https://www.thehotline.org/plan-for-safety/create-a-safety-plan/

Haven
https://www.haven-oakland.org/gethelp

Sojourner House
https://www.sojournerhouse.org/get answers

California Courts
https://www.courts.ca.gov

16 Steps to Support a Survivor
https://www.joyfulheartfoundation.org/6-steps-to-support-a-survivor

Friends & Family Guide
https://wscadv.org/resources/friends-family-guide/

Supporting Survivors: No More
https://nomore.org/learn/what-to-say/

Tipsheet: When Someone You Know is Being Abused
http://www.nationalcenterdvtraumamh.org/wp-content/uploads/2012/01/When-Someone-You-Know-is-Being-Abused.pdf

The Hotline: Supporting Others
https://www.thehotline.org/support-others/

Free Legal Aid

Domestic Violence and Sexual Assault State Coalitions
(many offer legal support)
https://www.domesticshelters.org/resources/state-coalitions

Guide to Domestic Violence Law in America
https://lawsuit.org/family-law/domestic-violence-law/

Find a Lawyer | Women's Law
https://www.womenslaw.org/find-help/nh/finding-lawyer

Legal Information by State | Women's Law
https://www.womenslaw.org/laws

Legal Momentum
https://www.legalmomentum.org

National Women's Law Center
https://nwlc.org/legal-assistance/

Preparing for Court / Forms | Women's Law
https://www.womenslaw.org/laws/preparing-for-court-yourself

Pro Bono Volunteer Guide by State | Pro Bono Net
This is designed for people seeking an opportunity for volunteering
in a legal project. https://www.probono.net/dv/oppsguide

State Legal Aid Resources
https://www.hirealawyer.findlaw.com/do-you-need-a-lawyer/state-legal-aid-resources.html

Women's Law
https://www.womenslaw.org/

Mental Health

"Dial 988 for Suicide and Crisis Hotline"
"Text HOME to 741741 for trained counselors at Crisis Text Hotline"

Find a Therapist "National Alliance on Mental Illness"
https://www.nami.org

Free Black Therapy
https://www.freeblacktherapy.org/

Mental Health America
https://screening.mentalhealthamerica.net/

Mental Health Resources | Mental Health First Aid
https://www.mentalhealthfirstaid.org/mental-health-resources/

Mental Health Resources for Black, Indigenous and People of Color
(BIPOC) | Mass General Hospital
https://www.massgeneral.org/psychiatry/guide-to-mental-health-
resources/for-bipoc-mental-health

National Institute of Mental Health
https://www.nimh.nih.gov/health/find-help

National Mental Health Organizations
https://www.nationalcenterdvtraumamh.org/resources/national-
mental-health-organizations/

Substance Abuse Mental Health Services Administration's National
Helpline https://www.samhsa.gov/find-help/national-helpline

The Holistic Psychologist
https://www.instagram.com/the.holistic.psychologist/?hl=en

The National Center on Domestic Violence, Trauma & Mental Health
https://www.nationalcenterdvtraumamh.org

The Secure Relationship
https://www.instagram.com/thesecurerelationship/?hl=en

The Mighty
https://www.themighty.com/

Very Well Mind
https://www.verywellmind.com/

Reproductive Rights

American Civil Liberties Union
https://www.aclu.org

Center for Reproductive Law and Policy
https://www.Crlp.org

Center for Reproductive Rights
https://www.reproductiverights.org

Four Women Health Services
https://www.fourwomen.com

Health and Human Services
https://www.hhs.gov

MSI United States
https://www.msiunitedstates.org

National Abortion and Reproductive Rights Action League
https://www.naral.org

National Association of Social Workers
https://www.Naswwi.socialworkers.org

National Women's Health Network
https://www.nwhn.org

Planned Parenthood
https://www.plannedparenthood.org

Prochoice America
https://www.prochoiceamerica.org

Sexual and Reproductive Justice Resources
https://www.nyc.gov

Text HOME to 741741, Trained Counselor at Crisis Text Hotline
988, Suicide and Crisis Lifeline

Education/Grants, Scholarships

American Association of University Women's Fellowships
http://www.aauw.org

Educational Grant | Live Your Dream
www.liveyourdream.org

Jeannette Rankin Women's Scholarship Fund
http://www.rankinfoundation.org/

Live Your Dream Awards
https://www.soroptimist.org/our-work/live-your-dream-awards/
index.html

Open Education Database
https://www.oedb.org/

Scholarships for Abused Women
https://www.scholarshipsforwomen.net/abused/

Women's Independence Scholarship Program
https://www.wispinc.org/

Education (Free)

Ask-Albert
https://www.ask-albert.com/online-degrees-us/o-tuition-online
Coursera
https://www.coursera.com

Common Searches
https://www.commonsearches.org

Duolingo-Learn a new language
https://www.duolingo.com

Education Connection
https://www.educationconnection.com

Free Code Camp
https://www.freecodecamp.org

Learn That
https://www.learnthat.com

Kadenza
https://www.kadenza.com

Harvard University
https://www.pll.harvard.edu/catalog/free

iResults
https://www.iresults.com

You Tube Educational Channels
https://www.youtube.com

Employment Resources

ACCESS
https://www.tributewebdesign.com/access/about-access.html

Career One Stop
https://www.careeronestop.org/

Dress for Success
https://dressforsuccess.org/

Skills to Get the Job
https://www.vtworksforwomen.org/programs/women/employment-support-services/job-skills

Reachire
https://www.reachire.com

Upwardly Global
https://www.upwardlyglobal.org/

Young Women's Trust
https://www.youngwomenstrust.org/get-support/

Women's Opportunity Center | Resumes & Cover Letters
https://www.womensopportunity.org/new-page-3

Women's Opportunity Center | Job Search Websites
https://www.womensopportunity.org/new-page-4

Women's Opportunity Center | Acing the Interview
https://www.womensopportunity.org/new-page-68

Workforce Innovation and Opportunity Act
https://www.dol.gov/agencies/eta/wioa

Financial resources:

Allstate Financial Literacy Program
https://allstatefoundation.org/what-we-do/end-domestic-violence/resources/

Jo Crawford

Clever Girl Finances
https://www.clevergirlfinance.com/

Financial Assistance for Food, Housing, and Bills
https://www.usa.gov/covid-financial-help-from-the-government

Free Stuff for Low-income Families
https://www.needhelppayingbills.com/html/get_free_stuff.html

Free Items on Craigslist
https://www.craiglist.com/

Freecycle Network
https://www.freecycle.org/

National Endowment for Financial Education (NEFE)
https://www.nefe.org/

Savvy Ladies
https://www.savvyladies.org/

Special Supplemental Nutrition Program for Women, Infants and
Children (WIC) https://www.fns.usda.gov/wic

Supplemental Nutrition Assistance Program (SNAP)
https://www.fns.usda.gov/snap/supplemental-nutrition-assistance-
program

Temporary Assistance for Needy Families
https://www.benefits.gov/benefit/613

Self-Care

Self-care is anything you do to take care of yourself, so you are
nourished on physical, mental, and emotional levels. Self-care isn't
only about easy and fun activities; it is also about the deep work
on healing trauma and rewriting your inner narratives and beliefs.

However, the intention is always the same. The work we do to take care of ourselves comes from the core belief that we are worthy of being healthy and happy. We are worthy of our own love, care, and affection.

45 Simple Self-Care Practices for a Healthy Mind, Body, and Soul
https://tinybuddha.com/blog/45-simple-self-care-practices-for-a-healthy-mind-body-and-soul/

Cory Muscara
https://www.instagram.com/corymuscara/?hl=en

Hey U Human
https://www.heyuhuman.com/quicklinks-ig/

How to Start Regulating Your Nervous System
https://www.healyournervoussystem.com/nervous-system-regulation-how-to-start-regulating-your-nervous-system/

Mental Health and Wellness Tools| Kaiser Permanente
https://www.healthy.kaiserpermanente.org/health-wellness/mental-health/tools-resources

Nervous System Regulation - Dr. Linnea
https://www.instagram.com/healyournervoussystem/?hl=en

Resources for Self-Care
https://www.delraymedicalctr.com/patients/our-response-to-covid-19/resources-for-self-care

Self-Care Guidance and Suggestions
https://www.shorturl.at/uVo28

Self-Care Questions
https://www.shorturl.at/lnrtv

Tiny Buddha
www.https://www.tinybuddha.com/

The Importance of Self-Care | Ted Talks
https://www.ted.com/playlists/299/the_importance_of_self_care

Why You Need a Self-Care Plan | Mindful
https://www.mindful.org/why-you-need-a-self-care-plan/

Zen Habits
https://www.zenhabits.net/archives/

Mindfulness & Breathing

Black Girls Breathing
https://www.blackgirlsbreathing.com/

Calm
https://www.calm.com/
Free Audio Meditation

https://www.fragrantheart.com/cms/free-audio-meditations

Getting Started with Breathwork
https://www.soulbody.co/blog/get-started-with-breathwork

One Love
https://www.joinonelove.org

Guided Meditation for Beginners from Quiet Kit
https://www.quietkit.com/

Insight Timer
https://www.insighttimer.com/

Center for Mindful Self-Compassion
https://www.centerformsc.org

Quiet Mind Cafe
https://www.youtube.com/channel/UCf-nkEuAif3R1Lt4JKnoigw

Self-Compassion
https://www.self-compassion.org/category/exercises/#guided-meditations

Smiling mind
https://www.smilingmind.com.au/

Tara Brach
https://www.tarabrach.com/new-to-meditation/

The Free Mindfulness Project
https://www.freemindfulness.org/download

White Noise Apps
https://www.sleepfoundation.org/best-sleep-apps/best-white-noise-apps

Free Yoga Classes

Black Yogi Nico Marie
https://www.youtube.com/c/BlackYogiNicoMarie/videos

Do Yoga With Me
https://www.doyogawithme.com/

Echo Flow Yoga | Trauma-informed Yoga
https://www.youtube.com/c/EchoGieselWidmer

Hannah Uiri | Trauma-informed Yoga
https://www.youtube.com/c/HannahUiri

Yoga with Adriene
https://www.yogawithadriene.com/free-yoga-videos/

Journaling

10 Journaling Tips to Help You Heal, Grow and Thrive
https://www.tinybuddha.com/blog/10-journaling-tips-to-help-you-heal-grow-and-thrive/

60 Journal Prompts for Self-Love, Self-Discovery
https://www.inspacesbetween.com/wp-content/uploads/2013/10/60JournalPrompts.pdf

105 Writing Prompts for Self-Reflection and Self-Discovery
https://www.reflectionsfromaredhead.com/writing-prompts-for-self-reflection/

Art Journaling
https://www.mymodernmet.com/art-journal-ideas/

Benefits of Journaling for Mental Health
https://www.positivepsychology.com/benefits-of-journaling/

Bullet Journaling
https://www.buzzfeed.com/rachelwmiller/mental-health-bullet-journal

Burning Letters: The Therapy of Letter Writing and Letting Go
https://www.bestselfmedia.com/burning-letters-letting-go/

Gratitude Journaling
https://www.com/gratitude-journal/

Healing through Private Words
http://www.sharonrhoover.com/2015/03/18/journaling-healing-through-private-words/

How to Start Journaling and Keep at It
https://www.merakilane.com/journaling-mental-health-start-journaling-keep/

Science-Backed Ways To Use Writing As Therapy
https://www.mindbodygreen.com/articles/can-you-really-use-writing-as-therapy
Stress Journaling
https://www.socialwork.buffalo.edu/content/dam/socialwork/home/self-care-kit/exercises/stress-journaling.pdf

Physical Health

Darebee
https://www..com/workouts.html

MonikaFit
https://www.youtube.com/c/MonikaFitt

Studio Jibby
https://www.youtube.com/c/StudioJibby

Free App | Workout for Women
https://www.apps.apple.com/us/app/workout-for-women-fitness-app/id839285684

Pay It Forward Ideas

Random Acts of Kindness
https://www.randomactsofkindness.org/

25 Frugal Ways to "Pay It Forward" | Wise Bread
https://www.wisebread.com/25-frugal-ways-to-pay-it-forward

About Jo Crawford

Jo lives in Maine with her rescue dog Tinkerbell. She spends time with her two daughters and three grandchildren. She is a CNN Hero and AARP Purpose Prize Fellow. She continues to pay it forward whenever possible.

You can reach Jo at jo@ittakesawoman.net

Acknowledgments

———

This book took me a very long time to write. Even though I had helped thousands of women believe that they deserved their dreams, my dream of writing a book was too big for me to believe. Who was I to think I could write a book anyone would want to read? That is still up for debate.

Instead of writing, I read. I read books written by wise, empowered women who were living fearlessly. Therefore, my first thank you is for these women who changed my life and helped me begin my journey of creating my own dream. So, I give a special thank you to Brené Brown, Glennon Doyle, Mary Pipher, Gloria Steinem, and the many others I have quoted within this book's "Wise Words." Some of their books are in the suggested reading list. They were my mentors.

Maida Berenblatt, who helped with the title, and Nadine Nesbitt were the first to take my desire to write a book seriously.

I could not have written this book without the help of KN Literary Arts and Nirmala Nataraj, who saved me by introducing me to my writing coach and editor Parthenia Hicks. Parthenia saw a very rough beginning and forced me to write on a real schedule. She supported me every step of the way. I call this "our book" because it would not exist without her.

Ruth Anne Specht is a dear friend who read and reread the book each time I needed encouragement. Holly Moirs added her terrific editing ideas, and Gail Shapiro did even more with her proofreading. Michelle Balfour, Judith Sanvicente, and Kailey Urbaniak at Cascadia Authors Services brought the book to life.

I appreciate Marissa Oketayot, who has helped me with all things technical, creative, and organizational for 15 years.

Thank you all, and forgive me if I have forgotten anyone. I thank you too!

www.ingramcontent.com/pod-product-compliance
Lightning Source LLC
Chambersburg PA
CBHW020242130626
46549CB00005B/2019